VGM Opportunities Series

OPPORTUNITIES IN
DATA AND WORD
PROCESSING CAREERS

Marianne Munday

Revised by
Margaret Gisler

Foreword by
Susan Fenner, Ph.D.
Manager, Education and Professional Development
International Association of Administrative Professionals

VGM Career Books

Chicago   New York   San Francisco   Lisbon   London   Madrid   Mexico City
Milan   New Delhi   San Juan   Seoul   Singapore   Sydney   Toronto

Library of Congress Cataloging-in-Publication Data

Munday, Marianne Forrester.
    Opportunities in data and word processing careers / Marianne Munday; revised by
Margaret Gisler; foreword by Susan Fenner.—Rev. ed.
        p. cm.—(VGM opportunities series)
    Includes bibliographical references.
    ISBN 0-658-01643-1 (hardcover) ISBN 0-658-01645-8 (paperback)
        1. Electronic data processing—Vocational guidance. 2. Word processing—Vocational
guidance. I. Gisler, Margaret. II. Title. III. Series.

    QA76.25 .M863 2001
    651.8'023—dc21   2001026429

VGM Career Books
A Division of The McGraw·Hill Companies

1 2 3 4 5 6 7 8 9 0 LBM/LBM 0 9 8 7 6 5 4 3 2 1

ISBN 0-658-01643-1 (hardcover)
     0-658-01645-8 (paperback)

This book was set in Times by Publication Services, Inc.
Printed and bound by Lake Book Manufacturing

Cover photograph copyright © PhotoDisc

McGraw-Hill books are available at special quantity discounts to use as premiums and sales promotions,
or for use in corporate training programs. For more information, please write to the Director of Special
Sales, Professional Publishing, McGraw-Hill, Two Penn Plaza, New York, NY 10121-2298. Or contact
your local bookstore.

This book is printed on acid-free paper.

To Jim

CONTENTS

ABOUT THE AUTHOR

Marianne Munday received her B.A. from Rutgers University and an M.B.A. from Virginia Polytechnic Institute and State University.

This edition has been revised by Margaret Gisler, a freelance writer living in Carmel, IN.

FOREWORD

Technology has forever changed our world. It has created a new global marketplace and interconnected economies to the point that E-commerce is becoming the norm. We can purchase products, services, and advice on-line and conduct business at any time, from any place. We're no longer bound to an eight-hour workday or limited by the proximity of skilled candidates in our immediate area. We can process work 24/7 by crossing international borders and using cyberspace as the new business venue. We can talk to people around the world in real or asynchronous time. We can meet face to face without leaving our offices through the use of cameras mounted on PCs or chat via keystrokes.

We can moan that technology has drastically altered the way we work and the way we live . . . or we can rejoice that it has given us opportunities to enrich, expand, and innovate. We may all have different feelings about the new role technology is assuming in our lives, but no one can dispute that it is the driving force in the world today. Although it has made some equipment, tasks, and processes obsolete, it has created new ways of getting work done—better, faster, and cheaper. And, it has forever modified how we view the world and do our jobs.

Office professionals who experienced the first wave and became the primary users of technology in the workplace have seen their roles and contributions greatly modified and expanded. Rather than merely "supporting" an executive or a professional and doing work assigned to them, office professionals have mastered integrated technologies and created their own special professional niche. It's been called the *clericalization* of the professional staff and the *professionalization* of the clerical staff. Once, the role of administrative assistants was to answer phones, take dictation, type letters, file paper copies, and organize office space. Today, managers have access to sophisticated cellular and wireless communication systems to receive and send their own personalized voice-mail messages, use desktop and laptop PCs to draft and send their own electronic correspondence (often bypassing the administrative assistant completely), E-file documents, and create directories accessible to everyone in the company, and they are being held responsible for organizing their own time, schedules, and projects. In turn, the clerical staff is utilizing management skills such as negotiation, project management, meeting facilitation, delegation, Internet research, and developing multimedia presentations for themselves and others.

One office occupation most affected by the pervasive use of technology within administration services is information processing. It has become a highly regarded and challenging career because these workers support all office functions. They create, manage, interconnect, store, and retrieve business information and communication. Because this career choice requires extensive knowledge of integrated software applications and systems, workers must be highly skilled in software programs and understand the importance and the intent of the information they process. They key, format, and enhance information transmitted to them. They clarify data by inserting charts, graphs, photos, artwork, audio and video clips, and spreadsheets, to create multimedia documents and products. Many know the fundamentals of graphic design and layout, use voice-recognition software and optical scanners, and incorporate other evolving technologies. Today's information processors are expected to be proficient with various software applications and seamlessly integrate them into any assignment. While many workers process documents, such as letters and reports, and update case or patient files, others focus on brochure design, prepare text and video annual reports, create presentations for meetings and training sessions, and provide handouts and supplemental materials for participants.

Information processors may work in one department or have responsibilities for several areas. They may report to a single manager or support multiple principles. Some are assigned to project teams where they may have a specialized role, such as desktop publishing, or fulfill numerous functions as defined by the team. Others may work in centralized areas, either on-site or off-site in a special facility. Some have their assignments hand-delivered; others receive them by E-mail. Some processors have direct links to artists or outside contractors and send finished and approved projects to printers via E-attachments for final processing. Some may get promoted to the rank of information processing supervisor and are responsible for hiring, training, and overseeing the workflow of colleagues. At this level, they must know how to create a budget, credit costs to departments and accounts, determine billing rates, and manage their centers as if they were stand-alone businesses.

As you can see, the range of skills required for being an information processor increases with the level of responsibility assumed. The salary ranges are commensurate to the duties performed. There are many jobs available in a variety of settings, and companies are searching for talented and hard-working personnel with creative and innovative ideas on how to use the new technologies as they evolve.

I can't think of a more challenging and rewarding career for someone who values continuing education, is comfortable with technology, is highly motivated, and is focused on outcomes. These are the keys to a successful and lucrative future in the field of information processing.

Susan Fenner, Ph.D.
Manager, Education and Professional Development
International Association of Administrative Professionals

INTRODUCTION

Personal computers have drastically changed the way individuals and businesses perform daily operations. They have greatly improved the accuracy and efficiency of work over the past twenty years. Today, there are not many offices that don't have computers available to most, if not all, of their staff. Computers also are becoming more visible in homes across the country. Because of their efficiency and increasing affordability, computers continue to have a revolutionary effect on every aspect of our lives. Because computers are so pervasive today, we have taken them for granted. Everyday tasks such as paying bills, shopping, banking, and corresponding with friends now are done with either a few strokes on a computer keyboard or with the click of a mouse.

The same is true on the job. Office automation is defined as the use of computers in the workplace to improve productivity. This means using computers to perform complex as well as simple tasks. Office automation is very important to the survival, further improvement, and growth of business. Companies are forever searching for computer applications that will increase their office productivity. Use of word processing, data processing, spreadsheet, desktop publishing, and communications programs are just some of the ways computers help to accomplish that feat.

This book introduces you to the field of office automation and focuses specifically on word processing and the opportunities it presents. Today, word processing (or WP for short) is the most common and popular computer application used both by businesses and in the home.

Although the business world did not utilize the advantages offered by word processing until the 1970s, it has been around since the 1960s. And now, in the twenty-first century, word processing has become an exciting career choice offering several opportunities in virtually every business category. There is definitely a tremendous demand for skilled word processing professionals and WP equipment operators.

What exactly is word processing, and how is it used in business? What kind of careers can a WP professional expect? What kind of WP training is available and how effective is it? What are the best systems to learn if you are new to the profession? This book answers those questions, along with providing necessary career information. Whether you are considering a career switch or just entering the job market, this book will provide the information you need to decide if a position in the WP field is really for you. If you currently have a position in the word processing field, you will find helpful information on such topics as spin-off careers, continuing education, and advancement.

With today's technological innovations, the typewriter is virtually non-existent for office use. Given that fact, a working knowledge of word processing and all of its elements is important for anyone wishing to successfully compete in the world of business and office automation. Therefore, regardless of your chosen career path, take some time to learn about this exciting and greatly expanding technology.

CHAPTER 1

THE ORIGIN OF THE AUTOMATED OFFICE

Office automation continues to revolutionize the way companies run their offices. It involves the streamlining of office operations with the use of computers. It only makes sense that with constant technological innovations occurring, the business world would seek to maximize office productivity while minimizing the necessity for manual procedures. Because of this, more and more businesses are utilizing the advantages offered by the many technological breakthroughs happening all of the time.

The use of computers to streamline office procedures is not a new idea. As early as the 1940s, computerized (or electronic) machines capable of automatically storing, retrieving, and processing data were already in place and being used by some American businesses. These machines were called "data processors" because they were high-speed number crunchers capable of efficiently performing tasks such as payroll, accounting, and inventory control.

Today's data processing equipment is highly sophisticated, with the ability to compute huge and often complicated volumes of numerical data at rapid speeds. For most businesses, these computerized machines are standard tools that help them operate more efficiently, and, therefore, remain competitive.

Word processing, like data processing, is just one of many computer applications being utilized by businesses today. WP is a key aspect of office automation because it enables businesses to significantly improve their productivity. In a most basic sense, word processing entails giving computer capabilities to the office typewriter (although as you will see, WP is really much more than that). The result is faster, cheaper, and more effective written communications. For example, it has been estimated that the use of word processing systems can produce a 25 to 300 percent increase in the typewritten output of a typical administrative assistant, and the cost savings to businesses can be just as impressive.

More and more companies have weighed these benefits, and given the paperwork they produce and the cost of producing that paperwork, the demand for computer systems capable of processing huge volumes of words and data has skyrocketed.

INTRODUCTION TO WORD PROCESSING

Word processing is often defined as "automated typing." That definition, however, is far from complete. Today, the term "word processing" is used to describe an entire system of streamlined work procedures, automated and technologically advanced equipment, and skilled people.

At the heart of the WP system is the computer. Three main types of computer equipment are used for word processing: personal computers, dedicated word processors, and electronic typewriters. Today the computer has taken on most of the functions of word processors and electronic typewriters, though many offices continue to make use of them in limited capacities. Personal computers use programs or software to perform word processing. Dedicated word processors are computers that do only word processing. They generally have built-in word processing software. Electronic typewriters look like electric typewriters but have a built-in dedicated computer that provides limited word processing capabilities.

Although word processing systems are often described as advanced versions of the standard office typewriters, they differ in a number of important ways. Personal computers and dedicated word processors display characters on a computer screen as the user keys them. Words, lines, paragraphs, even whole pages can be added, deleted, moved, or copied with a few keystrokes or the click of a button on a mouse. These systems check for spelling errors, and most are also capable of checking grammar.

At the touch of a key, the user can print out whatever has been recorded over and over again, allowing the creation of any number of freshly typed "originals." The user can then store the document on a disk or the hard drive, making it possible to produce additional copies or corrections at a later time.

ORIGINS OF OFFICE TECHNOLOGY

It is not surprising that office technology has advanced to this level of sophistication. The human race has been trying to perfect the art of written communication for thousands of years. Primitive cave paintings dating back more than 22,000 years have appropriately been described as "prewriting." They represent the first known attempts to communicate ideas without the aid of speech.

By 3,000 B.C. the Sumerians were using a much more advanced system of written communication. To improve record keeping, the Sumerian high priests began to inscribe business, legal, and historical information on clay tablets. Were these the rudiments of word processing? Probably so! Over time, the clay tablets that the Sumerians employed to record their writings were replaced by wood, papyrus, parchment, and eventually the high-quality paper that we use today. The stylus gave way to quills and finally to pen and ink.

Other advances that have had a significant impact on the evolution of written communications include the development of the Greco-Roman alphabet, which is still used today, and Johannes Gutenberg's invention of movable type in 1456, which made it possible to duplicate and mass produce written material.

THE TYPEWRITER

One invention that had a great impact on office automation and word processing is the typewriter. The introduction of the typewriter virtually eliminated the need to copy out documents by hand, which for centuries had been the only means of mass production. With the typewriter, high-quality written work could be produced at much faster speeds.

The Invention of the Manual Typewriter

The invention of the typewriter is generally attributed to Mr. Henry Mill, an English engineer. He received a patent for his invention in 1714. Little is known about his typewriter, however, because no description or model of it has ever been found.

Throughout the 1700s and 1800s, many inventors in both the United States and Europe tried to develop a more practical, efficient, and inexpensive version of Mill's machine. In 1867 Christopher Latham Sholes, with the assistance of Carlos Glidden and Samual W. Soule, invented the first successful manual typewriter. Sholes's machine consisted of understrike type bars that registered an impression of the typed characters beneath the typewriter roller. In essence, the individuals who operated these machines typed "blind." Because the typewriter keys hit the underside of the roller, it was impossible for the typist to see his or her work until it was finished. (In the early days, most typists were men, primarily because of the lack of women in the workplace. Also, the typists *themselves* were originally called "typewriters," and their machines were called "typographers.")

In 1874 E. Remington and Sons, the gun manufacturer, began to market the Sholes typewriter. Although the public was initially skeptical of the machine, Sholes's typewriter eventually revolutionized the business world. Other companies soon began producing their own version of the typewriter. Even so, it would be several more years before the typewriter was truly accepted by the business community.

Improvements that aided in the typewriter's eventual acceptance included the invention of the shift key in 1878, which made possible the printing of both capital and small letters; complete visibility of writing in 1880; and the development of the tabulator in 1897, which allowed margins to be set. The first successful portable typewriter was marketed in the early 1900s. In the 1920s one of the first true ancestors of office automation was invented— the electric typewriter.

Electric and Automatic Typewriters

Although Thomas Edison received a patent for an electric typewriter in 1872, it was not until the 1920s that a feasible model was introduced. It was powered by an electric motor and was much more efficient than manual machines. In 1935 International Business Machines Corporation (IBM) introduced the IBM Electromatic, a more streamlined model that greatly increased typing speeds and quickly gained wide acceptance in the business community.

During this same period, businesses began to express the need for a typewriter that would automatically produce individually typed copies of a form letter while retaining the appearance of the hand-typed original. The automatic, or repetitive, typewriter was developed in response to this need. This machine operated on the same principle as the player piano. Letters were code-punched onto a roll of paper tape. The perforations on the paper tape activated the typewriter keys and could be used over and over again to produce multiple copies of form letters.

Over the years manufacturers offered many improvements to both the electric and automatic typewriters. During the 1960s IBM led the field with a number of exciting innovations. In 1961 the company introduced the Selectric typewriter, an electric typewriter that operated without a movable carriage. Instead, the machine employed a removable typeball, or element, that contained all the letters and symbols found on standard typewriter keys. This revolving ball could print letters much faster than single-strike typewriter keys. The IBM Selectric was soon the most-used typewriter in the world.

IBM's MT/ST—The First Text Editor

Although the IBM Selectric was considered a major innovation, it enabled typists only to transfer words onto paper. Since it contained no corrections feature, text editing still had to be done using traditional methods—retyping, erasing, cutting, and pasting. But those days were soon over.

In 1964 IBM combined the features of the Selectric with a magnetic tape drive and introduced the MT/ST, the Magnetic Tape/Selectric Typewriter. Heralded as the first electronic text-editing typewriter, the MT/ST changed the whole concept of typewriting. In fact, with the development of the MT/ST, the age of word processing had truly begun.

The MT/ST was a hard-wired machine. That is, all of the functions of the machine were coded on internal circuit boards. The MT/ST was attached to a console containing magnetic tape, as opposed to slower, nonerasable paper tape. With this combination, it was now possible to edit and revise documents. The magnetic tape stored text and allowed the typist to record over any errors. The tape could be used over and over again to produce flawless copies of documents. However, although the MT/ST was far superior to its predecessors, its editing capabilities were still greatly restricted by limited machine intelligence.

The term "word processing" has its roots in the development of the IBM MT/ST. Actually, "word processing" is the English translation of the German word *textverarbeitung*. The term was coined in the late 1950s by Ulrich Steinhilper, a German engineer working for IBM. Steinhilper used the term to explain his theory that organizations could handle their written communications in a more systematic manner if their typing equipment was placed in a central location. There operators could type (or process) words without interruptions, which would save organizations both time and money.

In 1964 IBM again used the term to market the MT/ST as the world's first "word processing" machine.

GROWTH OF WORD PROCESSING

Following the invention of the MT/ST in the 1960s, the concept of word processing grew rapidly. Dozens of manufacturers joined the trend, producing increasingly sophisticated word processing equipment. One of the most exciting innovations was the introduction of microprocessors, or small computers, into the word processor. Microprocessors greatly expanded the machine's work capacity and allowed it to handle much more sophisticated text editing and formatting programs. The age of truly "intelligent" typewriters had arrived.

RECENT INNOVATIONS

More recent innovations include computer monitors that allow the user to view "soft copies" of his or her work. Zip disks are slightly larger than ordinary 3.5 floppy disks, but they are capable of holding the amount of data that would fill seventy 3.5 floppy disks. For these disks a compatible disk drive is necessary. Many word processing systems have offered upgraded twenty-first-century versions of their programs designed to be more user friendly and to offer more features, such as the ability to access information through its program from Internet sources. This information can be used for research purposes or can serve to offer suggestions and/or instructions on ways to improve the efficiency of the program.

Word processing systems are a standard part of most offices. As personal computers have become commonplace, they are programmed to do many things in addition to word processing. Other popular applications include spreadsheets, databases, and desktop publishing. In the next several chapters, we will enter the world of office automation. Let's start by taking a more detailed look at what word processing is and what it can do.

CHAPTER 2

WORD PROCESSING IS CHANGING TODAY'S WORKPLACE

EVERYONE IS KEYBOARDING

Have you decided whether a career in word processing is for you? Before you do, you should get a good idea of the technology used in this career. Most businesses and a growing number of homes have word processing systems already in place. In order to compete in this exciting field, a working knowledge of its complexities is essential.

This chapter introduces a number of important word processing concepts:

- differences between the traditional document production cycle and the word processing document production cycle
- a working definition of word processing
- the basic components of word processing equipment, both traditional and high tech
- general categories of word processing equipment
- standard word processing functions
- user-friendly word processing equipment
- the role of word processing in office operations
- the advantages of word processing

With this background, you will be well on your way to understanding what word processing is and how it is used by businesses. And you will be one step closer to making an informed career choice.

DOCUMENT PRODUCTION
The Traditional Cycle

Computers and word processing systems still have not found their way into a few business offices. In these offices, the standard electric typewriter is the key piece of equipment used. All typed documents pass through the typewriter roller at least once, and often several times, on their way to final copy. Figure 2-1 depicts the traditional document production cycle.

Let's take a closer look at the steps in the cycle.

1. The author, or document originator, prepares a text to be typed by the administrative assistant. The text is delivered to the administrative assistant by means of dictation equipment, shorthand dictation, or longhand notes.
2. The administrative assistant types the text using the office typewriter. As he or she depresses the typewriter keys, the characters are immediately typed out on a piece of paper. The administrative assistant reviews the completed text for typographical errors. If any are found, they are corrected by erasing, cutting and pasting, using white paint, or, in many instances, by completely retyping the document.
3. The text is returned to the document originator for approval.
4. The document originator proofreads the document and notes any necessary corrections or revisions.
5. If there are changes to be made, the document is returned to the administrative assistant.

Figure 2-1. Traditional Document Production Cycle

1. Author prepares
   text for typing.

2. Administrative assistant
   types document.

3. Document returned
   for approval.
4. Document proofread.
5. Revised document
   returned to administrative
   assistant for retyping.

6. Administrative assistant
   retypes document.

7. Retyped document returned
   to originator for more
   revisions (step 5) or
   final approval.

6. The administrative assistant makes the necessary changes. This may require retyping all or large parts of the original document.
7. After all the changes have been made, the revised document is returned to the document originator.

Steps 5 through 7 can be repeated as many times as necessary to produce a satisfactory final document.

As you can see, there are glaring inefficiencies in the traditional document production cycle. The administrative assistant often spends an exorbitant amount of time making revisions to the original document. In many instances, the changes are so numerous that the entire document must be retyped. Because of these inefficiencies, administrative productivity is much lower than it should be. The majority of the day is spent retyping and making corrections.

In addition, each time that all or part of a document is retyped, new typing errors are possible. Therefore, each new copy must be carefully and completely reviewed by the document originator or a qualified proofreader, a time-consuming and expensive effort.

The Word Processing Cycle

With the implementation of word processing systems, these types of inefficiencies can be minimized. Figure 2-2 shows a typical word processing document production cycle.

Let's look at the steps in the cycle in more detail.

1. The document originator prepares a text for keying into the word processor. The text is delivered to the word processing equipment operator by means of dictation equipment, shorthand dictation, or longhand notes.
2. The WP operator transcribes or records the dictation onto the word processor. As the document is typed into the system by means of the keyboard, it immediately becomes

Figure 2-2.   A Typical Word Processing Document Production Cycle

1. Document originator dictates text or actually types text directly into the computer.

6. Document originator approves or revises document. If revisions are needed, document is returned to WP.
7. WP operator recalls document and keys in changes only.

2. WP operator transcribes dictation onto word processor.
3. WP operator checks text on the monitor for errors and makes corrections.
4. Operator stores the document in WP equipment's storage system.
5. Text is printed out and returned to document originator.

8. Revised document is returned to originator for more revisions (step 6) or final approval.

visible on the monitor. This allows the operator to see and correct any errors *before* the document is printed out.

3. The WP operator checks the text on the monitor for errors. If there are any, the operator types, or *keys,* the changes into the system, and the revisions appear on the screen.

4. The WP operator stores the completed document on the WP equipment's storage system or on disk.

5. The text is printed out and returned to the document originator for approval.

6. If there are still changes or corrections to be made, the document is returned to the WP operator.

7. The original document is recalled from the word processor's memory and appears on the monitor. The WP operator makes all changes to the original document by means of the keyboard. *Note: Only the changes need to be keyed in. The entire document does not have to be retyped.*

8. After all changes have been made, the revised document is printed and returned to the document originator.

Steps 6 through 8 can be repeated as many times as necessary to produce a satisfactory final copy. Document revisions require very little operator time with word processing equipment. The bottom line is that in most offices, document production improved considerably with the introduction of word processing systems.

Personal computers have become the norm in most offices, and many professionals and managers now use desktop personal computers or workstations to enter data and do their own word processing. As this trend continues, the demand for typists, word processors, and data-entry operators will decline. Offices will continue to restructure and work roles will continue to be redefined as technological advances result in significant productivity gains.

A WORKING DEFINITION OF WORD PROCESSING

As our discussion of document production shows, word processing systems have a tremendous impact on office productivity. Word processing contributes to the production of written communications at faster speeds, lower costs, and with greater precision than methods used by most traditional offices. These are exciting claims and, as you will see, they are easily verified.

What exactly is word processing? Definitions range from simple to intricate. In fact, if you ask ten different people to define word processing, you will probably get ten different definitions. However, most office automation experts agree that the word processing concept encompasses much more than the WP equipment itself. The *Complete Office Handbook,* second edition, by Jaderstrom, Kruk, and Miller, defines word processing as:

> The single most commonly used PC application. A word processing program allows the user to enter, edit, and print text documents, such as letters and reports. The functions available in a word processing program will vary, depending on the brand and cost of the software as well as the size of the machine's memory.
>
> The following list is some of the basic features that a word processing program may include:
>
> Drag and drop editing
> Cross-platform compatibility
> Envelope printing
> File conversion
> File management
> Format templates
> Grammar and spell checkers
> Headers/footers
> Help feature
> Hyphenation feature

Index generation
Integration with spreadsheets, graphics, databases
Macro capabilities
Mail merge
Modular installation
Most recently used file list
Outlining
Paragraph and character styles
Shrink-to-fit previews and printing support
Special characters and symbols
Style gallery
Style sheets
Tabbed dialog boxes with preview windows
Table of contents generation
Text wrapping (automatic)
Thesaurus
Wizard assistants
Word, character, and line counting
Zoomable editing views

This definition and its components will form the basis for our discussion of the word processing concept. We will be viewing word processing as a system composed of three integral parts: people, procedures, and equipment.

The Word Processing Team

Successful word processing is a team effort. The word processing team is made up of a variety of trained professionals. The principals are individuals who originate documents for input into the WP system. We often refer to the principals as authors or document originators. Principals must have a good working knowledge of their company's word processing procedures in order to use the system efficiently and effectively.

WP operators run the word processing equipment, and they may also be principals. They are responsible for keying data into the word processor. WP operators work closely with principals and other WP personnel in the organization, including WP supervisors, managers, proofreaders, and trainers.

In addition, various support personnel help ensure the successful operation of the word processing system. Support personnel include equipment service technicians, trainers, systems analysts, salespeople, and many others.

Word Processing Procedures

Most organizations have developed standard procedures for the use of their computer equipment. These procedures describe how the word processing system is to be used by organization members and how work is to be completed by the WP staff.

Some businesses develop centralized word processing centers, like those envisioned by IBM's Ulrich Steinhilper. These centers concentrate the WP equipment in a production environment where it can be used most efficiently. Other businesses find that a decentralized word processing structure better meets their document production needs. (See Chapter 3 for a detailed discussion of word processing organizational structures.)

Regardless of the organizational structure, specific procedures regarding the origination and processing of documents must be developed and adhered to by all members of the organization. This ensures that document production is systematic and that the word processing system is being used to maximum advantage.

Word Processing Equipment

The computer is the key piece of equipment in any WP system. Like the standard office typewriter of years past, the word processing system's primary function is to produce typewritten documents. Unlike the standard typewriter, however, the computer has an internal memory that enables it to record and store information and later retrieve and manipulate that information.

Today, hundreds of computer systems with word processing programs of varying levels of sophistication are on the market. Although the systems may look different from one another, and may offer special features, they must perform five basic functions: data entry, data storage, data retrieval, editing, and printing.

To better understand each of these five functions, let's take a closer look at the basic components that make up word processing systems.

BASIC COMPONENTS OF WORD PROCESSING SYSTEMS

Most word processing systems have several basic components:

The CD-ROM.   The CD-ROM is a disk, similar to an audio CD, that contains files and programs. A standard CD-ROM can hold approximately 650 megabytes, or the equivalent of 250,000 pages of double-spaced typed text.

The CD-ROM drive.   This part of the computer is where a CD-ROM is inserted. It is then read by the computer for instructions.

The computer.   The computer is a machine that processes data with incredible accuracy and speed. Data are processed through the computer's ability to create it, reorganize it, display it, store it, calculate with it, and communicate with other computers. Computers also can process words, numbers, moving pictures, still pictures, and sounds.

The floppy disk.   The floppy disk is a thin, flexible, 3.5-inch, magnetically coated plastic disk. It is used to store data in digital form to be used at a later time and to send data from one computer to another.

The floppy disk port.   This part of the computer is where a 3.5-inch floppy is inserted. It is commonly referred to as the "A" drive.

The keyboard.   The keyboard is the place on the computer where you enter data into the system. The keyboard is similar to that of a standard typewriter; it contains all the same letter keys, in the same order as on a typewriter. However, the computer keyboard also has some additional keys, called command keys, that enable you to give the machine specific instructions such as delete, insert, move text, store, search, and print.

The monitor.   The monitor is a device that is usually attached to the keyboard. It looks and operates much like a television screen. It allows you to see a "soft copy" of your text as it is typed into the computer, before a hard copy is printed out.

As you key data into the computer by means of the keyboard, the corresponding characters immediately appear on the monitor. Once they are visible, you can manipulate them by using your command keys. You can change characters, move them around, adjust them, or delete them. This is possible because you are working with electronic images as opposed to physical images composed of ink on paper.

A process called "scrolling" allows you to retrieve and see data that are not currently displayed on the monitor. With the touch of a button, you can move text up and down, or left and right, to view and work with any portion of the text already entered into the WP system.

The mouse.   A mouse is a small, palm-sized device used by computer operators and manipulated with a mouse pad on a flat surface. A mouse is primarily used to give commands to a computer and move the insertion point. On top of the mouse are right and left click buttons that send commands to the computer.

The mouse pad.   A mouse pad is a smooth usually square mat that sits under the computer's mouse. This allows the mouse to move in a fluid motion, which is necessary for the mouse to function properly.

The speaker.   Computer speakers similar to those on small audio devices are used to process and play sound files and CDs with audio requirements.

The internal computer.   Today, personal computers are the primary tool used to perform WP functions.

The microprocessor is the central processing unit (CPU) in the computer. It is often called the computer's "brain." It is the internal part of the computer equipment that is responsible for processing, storing, and retrieving data from memory. The microprocessor performs all the mathematical and logical operations that keep the system running.

The other component of the internal computer is the memory. The computer has two types of memory: ROM and RAM. ROM, or read only memory, is the equipment's permanent memory. It stores the machine's operating instructions, which tell the CPU how to perform various functions.

Any text that you type into the computer using a word processing program goes into the RAM, or random access memory. This memory temporarily stores and handles all information that you give to the computer, and can later be erased. It is important to remember that random access memory is temporary; it depends upon electric power. If the equipment loses power, the information in RAM is permanently lost. For this reason, WP operators routinely store their work on external storage devices, disks, and CD-ROMs for later use.

The external storage system.   The computer's external storage system includes external storage devices, such as disks, CD-ROMs, tapes, and the storage media used to record the data on those devices.

External storage devices permanently record and store data keyed into the word processing system. Forms of external storage include floppy disks, magnetic cards, magnetic tape, and paper tape. Floppy disks are the most popular form of storage. Although the disks appear to be square, inside the disks are flat, circular, magnetic storage devices that are rotated like phonograph records by the system's disk drive.

Documents are stored on storage devices as "files." A file is defined as a "set of related information stored on a tape or disk." For example, this book was written with the aid of a computer, and each chapter was stored as a separate file on a floppy disk.

External storage devices are important because they allow WP operators to permanently save their work. This eliminates the need to rekey text each time you want to work with it and allows documents to be reprinted with speed and accuracy.

In addition to floppy disks, the external storage system includes the storage medium—the part of the computer that actually holds the storage device. The storage medium records data on—or reads data from—the storage device. For example, a floppy disk (storage device) is placed in a disk drive (storage medium). The disk drive either reads data stored on the disk or writes new information onto the disk.

The printer.   The printer produces hard copies of your data. That is, it transforms your electronic data into ink on paper. The computer printer is generally used only *after* the document is completed, rather than at each stage of the production process.

Printers can be classified as either impact or nonimpact. Impact printers transfer characters onto paper by means of an object striking an inked ribbon. Daisywheel printers and dot-matrix printers fall into this category. Nonimpact printers transfer characters onto paper without striking an object against the paper. Instead, characters are formed by heat, electrical charges, or inkjet (the spraying of ink onto paper). Laser printers are one type of nonimpact printer.

CONFIGURATIONS OF WORD PROCESSING SYSTEMS

The basic components of word processing equipment can be configured in a number of different ways. The five most common configurations, or categories, of word processing equipment are electronic typewriters, stand-alone word processors, shared logic systems, distributed logic systems, and personal computers with word processing capabilities. If you are familiar with the specific characteristics of each equipment category, you will find it much easier to identify and evaluate alternative word processing systems.

Electronic typewriters. Electronic typewriters, also known as low-level word processors or intelligent typewriters, are the most basic type of word processing equipment. They contain a microprocessor, limited memory, and some additional keys that make it possible to perform basic editing and formatting tasks.

Electronic typewriters have replaced standard typewriters at many administrative workstations. These intelligent typewriters have some important advantages: they are relatively inexpensive, easy to learn and operate, and can perform simple text editing and formatting functions. On the negative side, limited memory capacity, inability to do complex editing, and single or double-line video displays (as opposed to full video display monitors) make these machines inadequate for many business applications.

Stand-alone word processors. These systems are totally self-contained units. That is, they can function on their own without the assistance of another computer. There are two types of stand-alone word processors: blind stand-alone systems and stand-alone display systems.

Blind stand-alone systems consist of a keyboard/printer, internal computer, and a storage system. They do not have a monitor.

Stand-alone display systems consist of all of the above plus a monitor, which allows the operator to see what is being typed before it is printed out. The printer is generally separate from the keyboard.

Shared logic or cluster systems. These systems consist of several WP terminals that share the storage and processing power of one central computer. Unlike stand-alone systems, shared logic terminals are essentially "dumb." That is, they do not have their own internal computer, so they must be hooked up to a central computer in order to operate. These systems are often found in large offices where a number of word processing terminals can be linked to the central office computer, and, in some instances, to centralized disk drives and printers.

Shared logic systems represent a growing portion of the WP equipment market. A major advantage of these systems is that individual terminals can communicate with each other, which means that long typing jobs can be shared among several operators. One potential pitfall of shared logic systems is that all of the terminals rely on one central computer. If the central computer system malfunctions, all of the terminals will, as a consequence, become inoperative.

Distributed logic systems. These systems combine the best features of stand-alone and shared logic word processing systems. Like shared logic systems, distributed logic systems are made up of several WP terminals that share computer power, storage, and printers and that can communicate with each other. However, unlike shared logic systems, individual terminals do have some intelligence of their own; they are capable of operating independently of the central computer.

Personal computers.   Personal computers are the most powerful and versatile of the word processing machines. In addition to word processing, they can be programmed to do many other tasks, including data processing, desktop publishing, and communicating with other computers.

STANDARD WORD PROCESSING FUNCTIONS

Word processing systems perform two basic kinds of functions: editing and formatting. Editing functions allow text to be keyed into the system and then revised. Formatting functions make it possible to alter the physical appearance of a document, such as width of margins, line lengths, and page lengths. This section describes some of the more common editing and formatting functions and utilities.

Editing Functions

Cursor control.   The cursor is a small vertical line or character of light that shows you where the character you are about to type will appear on the monitor. As you type text into the computer, the cursor moves across the screen to show you where the next character you type will be located.

Once you have entered your text into the system, the cursor is also used to perform editing functions. Using the cursor control keys, the cursor can be moved up and down the screen, and left and right. By positioning the cursor at the point in the text where changes are to be made, you can manipulate (insert, delete, move) individual characters, words, or whole blocks of text.

Scrolling.   Scrolling refers to the upward/downward or left/right movement of text lines so that another section of the text is visible on the screen. This feature makes it possible to view an entire document that is too lengthy to fit on the screen at one time.

Word wrap. When typing on a standard typewriter, you must hit the return key when you reach the end of each line. The word wrap feature of word processing equipment eliminates this chore. Instead, the word processor automatically jumps to the next line when you reach the right margin. If a word is too long to fit at the end of a line, it is automatically moved down to the next line.

Insertion. The insertion feature allows you to add characters, words, phrases, paragraphs, and even pages in between other words or text. Insertions are made by moving the cursor to the position where you want to add something, giving the insertion command, if necessary, and then typing in the new text. The rest of your text automatically readjusts to make room for the new information.

Deletion. The deletion feature allows you to delete, or erase, characters, words, phrases, paragraphs, or even larger blocks of text. The surrounding text automatically readjusts itself.

Block movements. In word processing, a block refers to any amount of text that you designate as a block—a word, a sentence, a paragraph, a page, or more. The block movement feature allows you to define a block of text by marking its beginning and end with the cursor. Once you have defined a block of text, you can manipulate the entire block at once. You can move it to another location in the text, delete it, or duplicate it.

Search. The search feature allows you to look for a word, or group of words, that appears in the body of your document. After your computer has been told what word or words to search for, it scans the text until it finds the words in question, and then displays them on the monitor.

Find and replace.   This feature allows you to search for a word, phrase, or sentence in your document and replace it with another. For example, suppose you discover that you have misspelled one word consistently throughout your document. The find and replace function allows you to quickly search for each misspelling and to replace it with the correctly spelled word.

Spell check.   It is common for word processing programs to have their own internal dictionaries. The dictionary feature is used to check the spelling of each word in a document against the spelling in the dictionary. Misspelled words are highlighted on the monitor and are corrected either by the operator or automatically by the computer.

Formatting Functions

Setting margins and tabs.   Before you begin keying your document, you can set your right and left margins. The word processor is then programmed to type only within that space, and it will automatically move to the next line when you reach the right margin. It is also possible to set tabs at various locations on a line.

Justification.   On a standard typewriter, the left margin is always automatically aligned. The justification feature of the word processor allows you to have perfectly aligned left and right margins. In order to "justify" the right margin, the word processor inserts spaces of various sizes between words on each line so that all lines appear to be the same length.

Centering.   This feature makes it possible to center a word, line, page, or even an entire document automatically. It is usually accomplished by inserting spaces at the beginning of a line. Centering is particularly useful when preparing charts, because you do not need to count characters and spaces.

Hyphenation. With this feature, the word processor can automatically hyphenate a word that is too long to fit at the end of a line. The hyphenation feature is often used along with the justification feature to produce a perfectly aligned right margin.

Headings and footings. Headings and footings are words or phrases that appear at the top and/or bottom of each printed page of your document. The automatic heading/footing feature lets you type the repetitive words only once and then have the word processor print them on every page. For example, when this book was being prepared for the publisher, the author's name had to appear at the top of each page of the original manuscript. With a word processor, it had to be typed only once because the system was programmed to place the name as a heading on each page.

USER-FRIENDLY EQUIPMENT

The term "user-friendly" accurately describes much of the computer equipment being marketed today. The designers of WP systems are constantly upgrading their products to make them more friendly. This means that the equipment is getting easier to operate all the time. For example, many machines now understand commands that are in plain English (such as delete, insert, move) as opposed to commands in "computerese."

In addition, it is not necessary to understand all of the internal intricacies of WP equipment in order to operate it. A basic knowledge of computer equipment and its capabilities will generally suffice. The more knowledgeable you are, however, the more marketable you will be.

THE ROLE OF WORD PROCESSING

Every business has its own particular reasons for investing in a word processing system. In this section, we will look at some of the more common word processing business applications. This list is not exhaustive, but is intended to make you aware of the variety of roles played by word processing systems in an office operation.

Text editing.   Most businesses turn out a variety of documents that go through a number of revisions before being finalized. Without a word processor, this can involve a seemingly endless cycle of typing, correcting, retyping, correcting, retyping. In the case of particularly long documents, the revisions process can be very tedious.

With a word processor, revisions can be made in a fraction of the time they would take on a standard typewriter. The WP operator accesses the appropriate file, which is then displayed on the monitor; keys in the required changes; and prints out the revised document. The result is faster turnaround time, which means greater productivity in the workplace.

Business documents that often require extensive text editing include proposals, manuscripts, long letters, handbooks, newsletters, project reports, promotional material, and technical manuals and reports, to name but a few.

Repetitive typing.   Most businesses also have a number of form letters or standard letters they use over and over again. The basic content of the letters remains the same, but the headings, salutations, and certain key phrases in the letters may change. Before the introduction of word processing, form letters had to be typed out individually or, more frequently, photocopied with the variable information typed in separately. This was a tedious process, and invariably, the difference between the keyed-in text and the preprinted text was quite noticeable.

Word processing allows businesses to permanently store form letters so they can be used frequently without having to be re-typed. When needed, a document is simply recalled from memory and appears on the monitor. Variable data are then inserted within the body of the text as necessary. For example, if a company wants to send a mass mailing to its entire customer list, all it has to do is prepare one form letter; the word processor automatically inserts variable names and addresses. The time saved is tremendous, and the quality of each letter is perfect.

Many businesses also have standard paragraphs, or even larger amounts of information, that they use regularly in their documents or correspondence. With word processing, such boilerplate information can be stored and easily inserted into the body of otherwise original documents.

List maintenance and column alignment. Every organization maintains lists of one sort or another. Among the more common are lists of customers, employees, files, indexes, inventories, parts, patents, phone numbers, products, and mailing addresses. Most of these lists need to be updated regularly if they are to remain useful. With a word processor, updates require very little time or effort. Merging stored mailing lists with form letters to quickly and economically produce mass mailings is one of the most cost-effective applications of word processing.

Tabular material—data that must be perfectly aligned in a document—is also easy to produce with a word processor. Financial reports, for example, often contain long, complex columns of figures. Word processing eliminates the difficulty associated with typing columns of data because it has features such as automatic centering and automatic tabbing. Some word processors also have a function that automatically aligns decimal points.

Math processing. Many computers contain mathematical support packages that are capable of performing calculations of numbers entered into the system. Some equipment is only capable of simple calculations, such as adding, subtracting, multiplying, and dividing. More sophisticated systems can perform a wide range of complex mathematical calculations.

ADVANTAGES OF WORD PROCESSING AND OFFICE AUTOMATION

What advantages do businesses derive from the use of word processing systems? Recent studies indicate that most businesses enjoy four major benefits from word processing and other automated systems:

- improved worker productivity
- more accurate, higher-quality written work
- faster turnaround time in document production
- reduced communications costs

Improved worker productivity.   Word processing allows businesses to properly utilize their most important resource—people. With word processing, document originators are able to use their time more efficiently and productively. Revisions can be made effortlessly; proofreading time is reduced dramatically, and, as a result, the quality and amount of written work produced increases. WP operators also become much more productive. Reports of increases in typewritten output range from 25 percent to over 300 percent.

More accurate, higher-quality work.   Word processing results in the production of documents that are error-free and uniform in appearance. Editing techniques such as erasing, using white paint, and striking over mistakes are no longer necessary or acceptable.

Faster turnaround time.   Because of the special editing and formatting features of WP equipment, operators can produce documents rapidly. Changes can be made quickly and typed out on high-speed printers. The result is faster turnaround time in the production of all typewritten communications.

Reduced communications costs. The cost of producing a typical one-page business letter on a word processor is minimal. When you consider the billions of letters that are produced by businesses each year, the cost savings associated with word processing can be enormous.

The bottom line is that the effective use of office automation systems results in increased organizational efficiency and reduced communications costs. These benefits allow businesses to be more competitive and to more effectively meet their organizational goals.

CHAPTER 3

IMPACT OF WORD PROCESSING ON THE JOB

With the use of word processing systems, the traditional office structure has become greatly affected. In this chapter you will learn about the way businesses have restructured themselves to accommodate word processing systems. You also will be able to examine the types of career opportunities that can result.

THE TRADITIONAL OFFICE STRUCTURE

In traditional offices, the administrative or executive assistant handles both administrative and keyboarding tasks on a routine basis. In general, a one-to-one relationship exists between the boss and the assistant. That is, each assistant works for one boss, as opposed to working for many individuals.

In this work environment, the assistant is expected to be a generalist, a jack-(or jill)-of-all-trades. Responsibilities can include, but are not limited to, keyboarding, taking dictation, proofreading, filing, handling mail, answering phones, and running errands. The amount of time spent on each of these activities will depend on the boss's workload and the nature of the business.

Obviously, this type of office arrangement can be very ineffi-cient. For example, the assistant often is interrupted by phone calls, visitors, and additional work requests from the boss while trying to type a "rush" document. At the other end of the spectrum, the traditional office structure can leave plenty of room for wasted time and boredom. In fact, it has been estimated that the average assistant spends about 15 percent of the day just waiting for work.

As office costs continue to increase, businesses must take a serious look at ways to cut expenses and increase productivity. Certainly, more efficient use of support staff, including assis-tants, would do much to meet these goals. As we have seen, word processing systems go a long way toward improving worker productivity and controlling office costs.

THE WORD PROCESSING ORGANIZATION

We have defined word processing as a system of trained per-sonnel, specific procedures, and automated equipment that pro-vides more efficient and economical business communications. When businesses first implement WP, they often need to do some internal reorganization to accommodate the new system of personnel, procedures, and equipment.

Each business develops a unique word processing organiza-tional structure to meet its own particular needs. As a result, WP structures are as many and as varied as the businesses that de-velop them. In most cases, however, the organizational patterns that evolve fall into one of three general categories: centralized word processing, decentralized word processing, and word pro-cessing adapted to the traditional office structure.

Centralized Word Processing

In a totally centralized word processing organization, WP equipment is concentrated in a central location that serves multiple departments or groups within the organization. With centralization, general assistants are replaced by two types of specialists: administrative specialists and correspondence specialists (whom we shall refer to here as word processing specialists).

Administrative specialists perform all nonkeying tasks for the organization, including file maintenance, phone work, scheduling appointments, researching data, and dealing with the public. In some organizations, they also may do a minimal amount of keying. Word processing specialists handle *all* office keyboarding tasks, using word processing equipment. Both groups share the work of many executives, instead of being assigned to one boss. Such specialization of functions is thought to increase productivity and to offer more clearly defined career paths for both administrative and word processing personnel.

In most centralized WP organizations, separate word processing and administrative support (AS) centers are established, as shown in Figure 3-1. The word processing center performs all of the keyboarding tasks for the organization. The administrative support center provides all other work support.

With this type of office structure, document production procedures must be revised. Figure 3-2 shows the reorganized flow of written communications when separate WP and AS centers are established. The new document production routine involves the following steps:

1. The administrative specialist in the administrative support center assembles materials for dictation.
2. The executive (or, in some instances, the administrative specialist) prepares the document using dictation equipment.
3. The dictation is received at the word processing center.
4. The word processing supervisor establishes priorities and assigns the work to one or more word processing operators.
5. The word processing operator keys the document into the word processing system. A hard copy is printed.

**Figure 3-1. Organization of Separate Word Processing and
Administrative Support Centers**

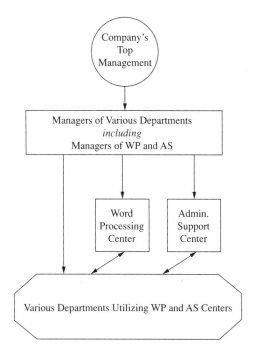

Figure 3-2. Organization of Written Communications with Separate WP and AS Centers

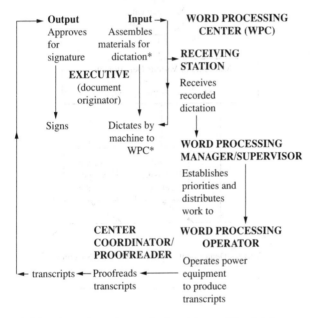

Administrative Assistant
in Administrative Support Center (ASC)

Output
Approves
for
signature

EXECUTIVE
(document
originator)

Signs

Input →
Assembles
materials for
dictation*

Dictates by
machine to
WPC*

**WORD PROCESSING
CENTER (WPC)**

**RECEIVING
STATION**

Receives
recorded
dictation

**WORD PROCESSING
MANAGER/SUPERVISOR**

Establishes
priorities and
distributes
work to

**CENTER
COORDINATOR/
PROOFREADER**

← transcripts ← Proofreads ←
transcripts

**WORD PROCESSING
OPERATOR**

Operates power
equipment
to produce
transcripts

*The administrative assistant also may be the originator of the dictation.

6. The document is proofread by a member of the word processing staff.
7. The document is sent back to the administrative specialist for preliminary approval.
8. After all necessary corrections have been made, final approval and sign-off are given by the executive.

In order for the system to work effectively, these standard operating procedures must be consistently followed by all members of the office staff.

Figure 3-3 shows a typical organizational plan for the word processing center in a large company. This company has both day and night word processing shifts to ensure maximum use of the equipment. The WP center is staffed by a variety of word processing specialists, including trainees, operators, proofreaders, trainers, schedulers, a supervisor, and a manager.

Because of constant technological innovations in the word processing industries, productivity coupled with office efficiency are always in high demand. Centralized word processing, although still used by smaller companies, is not as visible in larger business offices.

Decentralized Word Processing

In a decentralized word processing organization, smaller clusters of word processing equipment take the place of large, centralized WP pools. For example, a company may establish separate WP centers for each department or floor of the organization.

In a decentralized environment, administrative tasks may be performed by smaller administrative support centers, individual assistants, or a combination of the two.

Word Processing Adapted to the Traditional Office

A growing number of businesses are choosing to adapt their word processing systems to the traditional office structure. The

Figure 3-3.   Organization Plan for a Word Processing Center

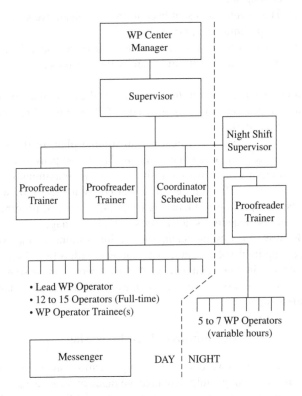

widespread availability of low-cost, multifunctional business computers has made it possible to locate equipment at individual workstations. Today personal computers can be found on the desks of assistants, managers, and various other support staff. As this trend continues, employment of word processing operators will decline. Job prospects will be greatest for those who are flexible and willing to continue to develop their skills. In particular, it will be important to know how to use a variety of computer software packages and have expertise with graphics, spreadsheets, and other computer applications.

WORD PROCESSING POSITIONS

There are numerous job opportunities for office workers who develop word processing and/or administrative skills. What jobs are available within a word processing organization? Just as there is no standard organizational plan for word processing organizations, there are no standard word processing job titles. This section will introduce you to common word processing positions. Chapters 4, 5, and 6 provide more detailed information on qualifications, training, and employment opportunities.

Word Processing Trainee

The word processing trainee generally has 0-12 months of word processing experience. The position requires typing proficiency (45 to 80+ words per minute), English grammar skills, and the ability to understand and work with sophisticated electronic machinery. The trainee learns to use the word processor to do simple correspondence jobs, such as recording routine transcription and playing out prerecorded documents. The trainee also may be responsible for logging production time and volume, and for some proofreading.

Word Processing Operator

The word processing operator, often called a word processing specialist, generally has a minimum of six months of word processing experience. In addition to carrying out all of the duties of the trainee, the word processing operator handles lengthier, more complex projects, and revises documents as necessary. He or she also has learned more advanced equipment and skills, and can assist other operators as needed. Familiarity with company terminology and document production procedures is necessary.

Word Processing Supervisor

The word processing supervisor generally has a minimum of two years of word processing experience and is a highly proficient WP operator. The supervisor is responsible for the day-to-day operation of the word processing center. This entails scheduling and coordinating the work, maintaining quality control, providing information to the rest of the company regarding the status of documents and workload, and identifying areas in the department for potential improvement. Some supervisors also may have some responsibility for budgetary concerns and equipment recommendations.

In larger companies, the word processing supervisor reports to the word processing manager.

Word Processing Manager

The word processing manager directs and controls the entire word processing operation. This involves developing procedures for word processing operations; selecting, directing, and guiding WP personnel; maintaining liaison with upper-level management; and designing word processing systems. In addition, the manager is responsible for the word processing budget, production reports, training schedules, and the coordination of activities within the administrative side of the organization.

Proofreader

The proofreader checks the keyed documents for spelling, grammar, and typographical errors. The job also entails keeping up-to-date on any special jargon or technical terms used by the organization. Proficiency in use of the English language and a keen eye for detail are essential.

Word Processing Trainer

The word processing trainer usually has a minimum of two years of word processing experience and is responsible for teaching new operators and others in the organization how to use the word processing system. The trainer also may instruct document originators in the use of dictation equipment and other procedures that help to ensure efficient use of the word processing system. The position requires superior equipment knowledge, an interest in teaching, and excellent communication skills.

Administrative Specialist

The administrative specialist generally assists two or more executives with day-to-day administrative details. The position involves little or no typing, but may include administrative support duties such as maintaining files, scheduling appointments, answering and making telephone calls, dealing with the public, and sometimes composing business communications. More specialized support can include research, mathematical calculations, proofreading, and editing.

The position requires organizational skills, tact, and diplomacy, as well as the ability to communicate with individuals at all levels of the organization. At a minimum, a high school education is required. College-level business courses are highly recommended.

CHAPTER 4

IS DATA/WORD PROCESSING FOR YOU?

Are you unsure whether a career in word processing and office automation is right for you? To help you answer that question, first take inventory of your individual skills, interests, and personality characteristics. Then use the information in this chapter to help you assess your potential for a satisfying career in word processing office automation. Specifically, this information includes:

- characteristics of the field
- employment outlook
- qualifications for word processing personnel
- what word processing operators like/dislike about their jobs
- working conditions
- salaries
- why you should learn word processing

WORD PROCESSING: A DYNAMIC, EXPANDING FIELD

If you are interested in a career in an expanding industry, you should carefully consider word processing. Sales of personal computer systems with word processing capabilities are booming. This translates into hundreds of thousands of word processing systems in the workplace, ranging from electronic typewriters to highly sophisticated word and information processors.

Why are businesses investing so heavily in word processing systems? In recent years, office costs have skyrocketed while worker productivity has remained relatively constant. In addition, due to the ever increasing need for more and better information, there has been a paperwork explosion in the workplace. In order to remain competitive in such an environment, businesses have had to look for ways to increase worker output and reduce costs.

Word processing provides these results. As we have seen, word processing helps control office costs, improves worker productivity, and makes it possible to disseminate information quickly and accurately.

Given these advantages, it is not surprising that most businesses already have invested in some type of word processing system, or plan to do so in the near future. As a result, there is a demand for word processing personnel who can maintain and operate those systems.

EMPLOYMENT OUTLOOK

According to the *Occupational Outlook Handbook,* the demand for keyboarders, word processors, and data-entry keyers is expected to decline through the year 2006, despite the ever increasing amount of information and business transactions sent and received. Ironically, this decline is a reflection of the increased worker productivity made possible by word processors. Technological advances in word processing allow fewer workers to handle a larger amount of work. In addition, personal computers have become the norm, encouraging many executives to key documents themselves rather than delegating all assignments to word processing personnel.

Despite these changes, there will be a continuing need for word processors to replace those who move on to other occupations or leave the workplace. This need is expected to create many thousands of word processing jobs each year. Strong technical skills and knowledge of more than one word processing "language" will increase your opportunities for employment in the field.

Historically, most positions in word processing were held by women. However, an increasing number of men are entering the field. Word processing offers both men and women an opportunity to be at the forefront of office automation. In addition, they find that a word processing background can be a stepping-stone to a wide variety of career options. Experienced word processing operators often go on to supervisory positions or other information processing careers.

QUALIFICATIONS FOR WORD PROCESSING PERSONNEL

As we have discussed, any successful word processing system includes professional people, WP equipment, and standard procedures. Although all three elements are essential, it is professional people who keep the word processing systems up and running efficiently. Without highly skilled personnel, word processing systems would be little more than masses of machinery.

Employers know that the selection of a good word processing operator can greatly improve office productivity and the quality of written work. On the other hand, the selection of a poorly trained operator can have disastrous effects on productivity, work quality, and office morale. Therefore, employers are very concerned about getting the best people to operate their word processing systems.

There are two categories of characteristics that employers look for in their word processing personnel: technical skills and personal traits. Technical skills include those office, language, and math skills that are necessary to be successful in the word processing field. Personal traits are those individual qualities that employers look for in a word processing professional. Take some time to review these characteristics and determine whether or not they describe you. Please note that, although the following discussion centers on the WP operator, these technical skills and personal traits are important for any position in word processing.

Technical Skills

Keyboarding skills. Aspiring word processing operators should be able to key quickly and accurately. Standards for entry-level word processing positions range from 45 to 80+ words per minute, depending on the nature of the work. Some employers stress keyboarding skills first and equipment knowledge second. Others are more concerned that you are able to operate their particular brand of equipment, and believe that keyboarding speed comes with experience on the equipment.

An interest in machines.   The ability to understand and work with modern, technical equipment is essential. Although most word processors are user-friendly, they are, without a doubt, more intricate than standard typewriters. You should enjoy the challenge of working with computerized equipment and be willing to do so on a daily basis.

English language skills. A strong command of the English language, including knowledge of English grammar and usage, is also imperative. Word processing operators should be able to produce documents that are free of grammar, spelling, and punctuation errors. In some instances, editing skills may be required.

The ability to read, follow, and interpret directions. Word processing operators should be able to read and interpret documents without constant supervision. Of course, questions should be asked if you are unable to interpret the document originator's work, but common sense should be used whenever possible.

Personal Traits

Professionalism. Professional word processing operators are resourceful, independent, and willing to take initiative. Professionalism also implies loyalty to your boss and enthusiasm about your work.

An interest in office automation. Operators should enjoy typing and working with modern equipment. This interest should translate into neat, accurate work in which both the employer and operator can take pride.

Dependability. A commitment to reporting to work as scheduled and on time is essential to efficient word processing operations. Absenteeism and tardiness create backlogs and place unnecessary pressure on both the employer and coworkers.

Ability to handle pressure. Operators must regularly cope with difficult assignments, deadlines, and changing priorities.

Pressures and frustrations are common in such an environment. However, WP operators must be able to handle these pressures with a positive attitude and patience.

Concentration.　Operators must sit at their word processing terminals for long periods of time. In fact, many operators spend 80 percent or more of the day at their equipment. The ability to concentrate and remain confined to one area is essential.

Human-relations skills.　WP operators must be "team players." They must be able to work well with principals, technicians, administrative assistants, and other members of the word processing team. A cooperative, helpful attitude can have a big impact on productivity and office morale.

Task-orientation.　The primary job of the word processing operator is to produce printed materials accurately and efficiently. Output is closely scrutinized, and the quantity and quality of that output can be easily measured and evaluated. WP operators must be able to perform well in this type of production environment.

Employers are always assessing the qualifications of their word processing personnel, as well as those of their other employees. Because personal traits are not easily evaluated, employers must make subjective appraisals of these characteristics. Technical skills, on the other hand, are much more easily measured. A variety of production-oriented techniques exist and are currently used by employers as skill evaluations. These techniques include line and page counts (to see how many lines or pages of text an operator produces in a particular period of time), turnaround time in producing documents, and error rates. As a WP operator, you should be ready to have your work scrutinized in this manner.

THE PROS AND CONS OF A JOB
IN WORD PROCESSING

A number of studies have explored how word processing operators feel about their jobs. What are some of the positive and negative aspects of their positions? A summary of that information follows.

Positive Aspects of Word Processing Positions

Most word processing operators agree that their positions offer the following:

1. An opportunity to learn how to operate and use sophisticated office equipment. WP operators are at the forefront of office automation. They develop technical skills that can be adapted to a variety of office equipment, including word processors, data processors, and multifunctional business computers.
2. The ability to produce higher volumes of work in less time than traditional typing methods. Substantial increases in productivity are reported by most word processing operators. Such immediate results make their jobs more rewarding and less stressful and free them to take on more challenging tasks.
3. Additional career opportunities because of word processing skills. With the right amount of training and experience, WP operators can go on to positions as WP supervisors, managers, and trainers. They also can use their word processing expertise to branch out into new careers in fields such as sales, computer programming, desktop publishing, and teaching. They often are able to

arrange flexible work schedules or assignments with temporary employment agencies.

4. An opportunity to work with a variety of professionals. WP operators work closely with principals and other WP professionals in the organization. They also come in contact with manufacturers' representatives.

5. A variety in the workload, which keeps them busy and interested. Because word processing makes operators more efficient and able to produce a higher volume of work, they often have time to take on a greater variety of work, which often involves more challenge and responsibility.

Negative Aspects of Word Processing Positions

Word processing operators do have some complaints about their jobs. These include the following problems:

1. Potential health hazards associated with using word processing equipment. Complaints range from musculoskeletal strain, headaches, backaches, eyestrain, and fatigue, to stress-related illnesses and carpal tunnel syndrome.

2. Excessive stress and job pressures. Some operators report that principals and WP supervisors have unrealistic expectations of the capabilities of the WP equipment. They therefore place unreasonable demands on operators, making their jobs stressful.

3. Being treated like a machine instead of a person. This is one of the biggest complaints of word processing operators. The intensive production orientation of some companies can translate into a lack of concern for the personal needs of WP operators. This lack of concern

can result in poor motivation, emotional and physical stress, and frustration among equipment operators.

4. Poor training on word processing equipment. Training programs offered by employers and schools vary considerably. In some instances, the training is inadequate, and operators are less productive as a result.

5. Lack of appreciation by supervisors and others. Some WP operators believe that their capabilities are unrecognized. They want to be told when they perform well and to be treated with respect and consideration.

6. Unfair work measurement techniques. Some word processing organizations closely measure and evaluate each operator's output and performance. Because the degree of difficulty varies from one assignment to the next, it can be unfair to use techniques such as line and page counts to compare and evaluate operators.

Certainly, the degree to which any of these problems exists varies greatly from one employer to the next. However, when evaluating any employer, try to determine if any of these problems is a potential concern. Spend some time talking with other members of the word processing staff. In most instances, they will be your most reliable source of information about working conditions at the company.

WORKING CONDITIONS

Today, manufacturers and employers alike are making every effort to provide a safe, comfortable work environment for word processing employees. The fact remains, however, that most word processing operators sit at a terminal for at least 80 percent of their workday. This has led to a number of health-related operator complaints.

Potential Health Problems

Monitor-related problems.   Recent studies have linked monitors to eyestrain, migraine headaches, nausea, lower and upper back pain, other musculoskeletal problems, and increased levels of job stress.

Job stress.   Quotas, difficult assignments, deadlines, and changing priorities all can take their toll on the WP operator. High levels of job stress potentially can lead to stress-related illnesses, including coronary heart disease.

Sitting for long periods of time.   Excessive sitting, combined with poorly designed chairs, can lead to backache and also can aggravate hemorrhoids, varicose veins, and other circulatory conditions.

Fatigue.   Intense concentration can lead to both muscular and mental fatigue.

Noise.   High levels of machine noise can be annoying and potentially harmful to hearing.

Carpal tunnel syndrome.   Excessive typing can cause pain and numbness in the wrists, palms, fingers, and thumbs.

The Solution: Ergonomics

Ergonomics is the application of biological and engineering data to problems pertaining to people and machines. In response to workers' complaints about health problems related to their word processing positions, WP equipment and furniture manufacturers are including ergonomic features in word processing workstations.

Ergonomic furniture has been designed to provide WP operators with more comfortable working conditions. There are now special chairs with adequate support and work surfaces that are the correct height. In addition, monitor screens that are flicker free and can be adjusted for brightness are standard. Some companies have had their monitor screens fitted with special filters designed to reduce glare. Adequate consideration also is being given to overhead lighting to minimize eyestrain. Printers are getting less noisy all the time, and most employers now make every effort to station noisy printers away from the word processing work areas.

Another recent innovation is the ergonomic keyboard. It is designed to pad the wrists while typing, which reduces the risk of the onset of carpal tunnel syndrome.

Employers have a responsibility to provide a suitable work setting for their employees. When evaluating a potential employer, consider the following:

- What types of word processing furniture are used? Do chairs give sufficient support to operators? Are desks the proper height and spacious enough to support work requirements? Can equipment height be adjusted?
- Are WP monitor screens flicker free? Is there proper overhead lighting?
- Are noise levels acceptable?
- Is an adequate number of breaks allowed? The National Institute for Occupational Safety and Health (NIOSH) recommends a fifteen-minute break every hour for individuals under high visual demands.
- Is the general environment favorable?

If you are satisfied with your answers to these questions, you may be on your way to a pleasant, new working relationship.

SALARIES

The word processing field offers attractive salaries. Certainly, your salary will be affected by the industry you choose, the company you work for, the region of the country you live in, and your experience and ability. On the average, however, you will find that word processing positions offer higher salaries than those found in more traditional office positions.

According to the Office Team administrative staffing division of Robert Half International, Inc., the average salary for a word processor is between $22,500 and $26,750. A word processor is defined here as someone who creates, edits, and proofs a variety of documents; transcribes tapes; and is proficient with the latest word processing software. Executive word processors will earn between $26,000 and $33,000. Their job will entail using word processing programs with an emphasis on advanced projects. They also will have the ability to use special features and adapt to unfamiliar systems with minimal review, as well as perform specialized functions such as graphics creation, troubleshooting, and integration of data from different software applications.

You also can get a better idea of the salary you can command by reading help-wanted ads in your local newspaper, talking with potential employers about the salaries they offer, consulting employment counselors/recruiters about your worth in the WP job market, and speaking with people already employed in your field of interest.

Of course, the more specialized training and experience you have, the more likely you are to surpass the WP salary averages.

WHY YOU SHOULD LEARN WORD PROCESSING

Whether or not you decide to enter the field, a working knowledge of word processing can be a long-term asset. On a personal level, the ability to use word processing equipment can save you considerable time when it comes to writing reports, keeping personal records, and even shopping and paying bills.

Professionally, word processing expertise can be a real advantage. As businesses become more computer-oriented, most positions will require some familiarity with this technology. You will be at the leading edge of the office automation revolution if you have a working knowledge of word processing equipment.

CHAPTER 5

PREPARING FOR WORK IN
AN AUTOMATED OFFICE

Today when most students graduate from high school, they are already proficient at keying information because of all the work that they have done on the computer, and they could get an entry-level position in an automated office. However, did you realize that if you complete an office administration program you will be even better prepared for an automated office environment? You will have developed basic office skills and acquired computer skills, including word processing, spreadsheet, database, and microcomputer operating systems. During your studies you will have the opportunity to learn several other applications like advanced word processing, desktop publishing, and integrated packages. Most office administration programs are designed to accommodate students with different levels of training experiences. You will find courses that provide initial, advanced, and refresher education and assist individuals in achieving professional recognition and career progression.

In addition, students who complete all the recommended sequences of courses are eligible to take the Administrative Information Processing Specialist (AIPS) or the Certified Professional Secretary (CPS) exams administered by the Institute for Certifying Secretaries of the International Association of Administrative Professionals.

59

Not so long ago, typists were in great demand because they were responsible for the production of most written communications in the workplace.

Training for a position as a typist was a relatively simple and straightforward process. Typewriters did not differ from one another very much. Therefore, it was possible to learn to type on equipment at virtually any high school, community college, secretarial or business school, or even at home, and easily transfer those skills to the workplace.

For proficient typists, employment opportunities abounded in practically every business category. And employers could easily determine proficiency. For example, if a 60+ words-per-minute typist was needed, the employer could sit applicants down at a standard office typewriter and test their skills.

Because of the proliferation of automated office equipment, the heyday of the conventional office typist who can only operate a standard typewriter is over. In fact, some job analysts have gone so far as to describe the conventional typist as an "endangered species."

In the present job market, word processing expertise is virtually a prerequisite for many office positions. Today, high school graduates often need to have technical skills such as word processing just to land an entry-level job.

Mastering the fundamentals of word processing is without a doubt more difficult than learning basic keyboarding skills. As we have seen, the capabilities of word processing equipment are far greater than those of a standard typewriter. Because there are so many word processing functions to be understood and mastered, it takes three to six months, typically, for a WP operator to become proficient on the equipment. Basic keyboarding skills can often be learned in as many weeks.

Even before an aspiring WP operator begins to train, there are numerous important decisions he or she has to make. With so many different systems to choose from, which system or systems should you take the time to learn? Having made that decision, where should you obtain your training? What constitutes good training?

These are all very important questions. Yet, there is no single correct answer to any of them. The purpose of this chapter is to provide you with the kinds of information you need in order to choose the training that is most appropriate for you.

DECIDING WHICH SYSTEMS TO LEARN

Which word processing system should you learn? This is a very important decision, as it will undoubtedly influence the kinds of jobs you will be qualified to perform. Some employers are only willing to hire WP operators who have been trained on their particular word processing system.

There are just too many systems currently on the market to be knowledgeable about each one. Therefore, you will want to learn the WP system that best matches your individual interests and needs. The following guidelines should assist you in making an informed decision:

- Familiarize yourself with the major components of word processing equipment, general categories of equipment, word processing software programs, and basic word processing functions, as outlined in Chapter 2. With this background, you should be able to knowledgeably compare alternative systems and weed out those that are incompatible with your needs.
- Study the job market that interests you. You will find that different industries prefer different types of systems. You can determine which system best matches your career objectives by talking to employment counselors, scrutinizing help-wanted advertisements (many ads now list the specific word

processing programs that operators will be using), talking to the personnel offices of companies you are interested in working for, and talking to WP operators currently employed in your field of interest.

EVALUATING TRAINING PROGRAMS

Although there are a variety of options to choose from, there is no single best way to obtain word processing training. Each type of training has advantages and disadvantages. Therefore, you should carefully consider each option available to you and pick the one that best suits your circumstances.

When evaluating your alternatives, consider the following factors:

WP equipment.   The facility you choose should train on state-of-the-art equipment that is being used in the job market that interests you. Make sure that there are enough machines to accommodate class size, and that you are given plenty of opportunity to practice on the equipment.

Teaching philosophy.   Ideally, your program should include a combination of *conceptual* and *operational* training. Conceptual courses teach the fundamentals of word processing—what it is, what its capabilities are, how it can be used to maximum advantage. Operational training teaches students how to operate the WP equipment.

Training environment.   Word processing is taught in a variety of settings: formal classroom instruction, one-on-one instruction, and informal group instruction. You should choose the training environment in which *you* feel comfortable. Do not settle for overcrowded classrooms, cramped work spaces, or an impersonal approach to teaching.

Course length.   Length of training can range from as little as two weeks to two or more years. The amount of education that you decide on should reflect the amount of time you have available and your long-term career goals. In all cases, evaluate course length to determine if there is adequate training time to meet your individual needs.

Job placement and internships.   Formal job placement programs and internship programs associated with training programs are becoming more and more common. If possible, choose a program that offers those added advantages.

TYPES OF TRAINING AVAILABLE

Once you have clarified your personal objectives, you are ready to learn word processing. Several common avenues of training are available to you:

- college-level training
- company-sponsored training
- word processing equipment vendor training
- business school training
- training through temporary help services
- training by independent consultants
- self-instruction

Unfortunately, there is no comprehensive list of training sources. Consult your phone book, the local library, and career guidance counselors for help in gathering this information. In addition, the International Association of Administrative Professionals (described in Appendix A) may be able to provide some assistance.

Let's take a closer look at some of the more popular training alternatives.

College-Level Training

Today, many word processing and information processing management positions require an advanced education. If you are looking to move into management, you will want a well-rounded educational background. Therefore, you should consider attending college.

Most community colleges and a growing number of four-year colleges now offer some word processing training. Some schools offer a few word processing courses; others have developed entire word processing programs. There are word processing certificate programs that average one year in length. There are also two-year associate degree programs that include a larger number of academic and office automation courses. Today, a four-year degree program, especially in business administration or business education, also can include word processing courses in its curriculum.

The following curricula are provided to give you a sample of the types of courses you might expect to take at the community college level.

A Typical Certificate Program (One-Year)

Students can earn a Technical Certificate–Administrative Assistant Specialty upon successful completion of thirty semester units of courses in the following areas:

General Education Courses	Credits
English Composition	3
Sociology or Humanities/Social Sciences Elective	3
	6

Technical Courses	Credits
Document Processing	3

Administrative Assistant Specialty Courses	
Word Processing Applications	3
Office Procedures	3
Introduction to Microcomputers	3
	9

Business/Office Courses	
Integrated Office Applications	3
Business Communications	3
	6

Electives	
Presentation Graphics	3
Multimedia Design	3
Computer-Operator Problem Solving	3
Spreadsheets	3
Co-Op Internship	3
Microcomputer Operating	3
	6*

* A minimum of two electives must be taken.

A TYPICAL ASSOCIATE DEGREE PROGRAM
(TWO-YEAR)

Students who complete sixty semester units in the following areas will earn an Associate of Applied Science and be able to get a job in one of the following areas:

ASSOCIATE OF APPLIED SCIENCE –
ADMINISTRATIVE SPECIALTY

General Education Courses	**Credits**
Fundamentals of Public Speaking	3
Economic Fundamentals	3
English Composition	3
Functional Mathematics *or*	
Intermediate Algebra	3
Physical Science or Life/Physical Science Elective	3
Sociology or Humanities/Social Sciences Elective	3
	18

Technical Courses	
Accounting Principles	3
Introduction to Business	3
Introduction to Microcomputers	3
Document Processing	3
Business Communications	3
Office Administration and Supervision	3
	18

Administrative Specialty Courses	
Word Processing Applications	3
Office Procedures	3
Desktop Publishing	3
Records and Database Management	3
	12

Business/Office Courses	
Integrated Office Applications	3
Advanced Document Processing	3
	6

Electives	Credits
Presentation Graphics	3
Multimedia Design	3
Computer-Operator Problem Solving	3
Spreadsheets	3
Co-Op Internship	3
Microcomputer Operating Systems	3
	6*

* A minimum of two electives must be taken.

ASSOCIATE OF APPLIED SCIENCE–LEGAL SPECIALTY

General Education Courses	Credits
Fundamentals of Public Speaking	3
Economic Fundamentals	3
English Composition	3
Functional Mathematics *or*	
Intermediate Algebra	3
Physical Science or Life/Physical Science Elective	3
Sociology or Humanities/Social Sciences Elective	3
	18

Technical Courses	
Accounting Principles	3
Introduction to Business	3
Introduction to Microcomputers	3
Document Processing	3
Business Communications	3
Office Administration and Supervision	3
	18

Legal Specialty Courses	Credits
Word Processing Applications	3
Introduction to Paralegal	3
Legal Research	3
Civil Procedures	3
	12

Business/Office Courses	
Legal Transcription	3
Advanced Document Processing	3
	6

Electives	
Presentation Graphics	3
Desktop Publishing	3
Integrated Office Applications	3
Multimedia Design	3
Computer-Operator Problem Solving	3
Spreadsheets	3
Records and Database Management	3
Co-Op Internship	3
	6*

* A minimum of two electives must be taken.

ASSOCIATE OF APPLIED SCIENCE–SOFTWARE SPECIALTY

General Education Courses	Credits
Fundamentals of Public Speaking	3
Economic Fundamentals	3

	Credits
English Composition	3
Functional Mathematics *or*	
Intermediate Algebra	3
Physical Science or Life/Physical Science Elective	3
Sociology or Humanities/Social Sciences Elective	3
	18

Technical Courses

Accounting Principles	3
Introduction to Business	3
Introduction to Microcomputers	3
Document Processing	3
Business Communications	3
Office Administration and Supervision	3
	18

Software Specialty Courses

Word Processing Applications	3
Desktop Publishing	3
Multimedia Design	3
Computer-Operator Problem Solving	3
Spreadsheets	3
	15

Business/Office Courses

Integrated Office Applications	3

Electives

Presentations	3
Office Procedures	3

	Credits
Advanced Document Processing	3
Records and Database Management	3
Co-Op Internship	3
Microcomputer Operating Systems	3
	6*

* A minimum of two electives must be taken.

TIPS ON CHOOSING A COLLEGE

- Determine the length of time and amount of money you will be able to spend on your education. This will help you determine whether you should look at community colleges or four-year programs.
- Contact the admissions offices of the schools that you are interested in to be sure that they offer word processing training. Ask for a catalog of courses and also ask to be put in contact with the department that offers word processing. They can provide you with more detailed information about their word processing program.
- Make sure that the word processing equipment being used is up-to-date and that word processing courses are well-rounded.
- Talk with students currently enrolled in the programs to determine if they are satisfied with their training.
- Evaluate job placement services and internship possibilities.
- Find out if you can enroll as a special student and take only one or two word processing courses or if you must enroll as a regular full-time student. You might want to start school on a part-time basis to evaluate the program and determine your interest in word processing.

If you are currently employed, find out if your employer will pay for you to take word processing courses. Many do. You might be able to start your college education on a part-time basis without having to leave your present job.

Company-Sponsored Training

If you are presently employed by a company that uses word processing equipment and you are interested in learning the system, you are probably in luck. Many companies train members of their own staff to become word processing operators. Assistants, keyboarders, and other staff members generally are chosen to learn word processing skills because of their familiarity with company policies and procedures, equipment, training techniques, and work schedules.

Like college-level programs, company training programs vary considerably. Some employers develop their own in-house training programs. These can range from formal classroom instruction to informal group classes to one-on-one instruction. Other companies use programs and materials developed by the vendor from whom they purchased their system. Still others bring in outside consultants to do the training, or even encourage employees to become "self-taught" operators by reading equipment manuals. Most companies use some combination of these training methods.

A major advantage of company training is that it is free to the employee, paid for by the company. In addition, company-sponsored training ensures that you are learning to use the specific kind of equipment that you will be called upon to operate in your day-to-day work.

Before committing yourself to a company training program, make sure that the training is adequate. This often can be determined by talking to other operators and to the manager who coordinates the training effort.

Equipment-Vendor Training

Many computer equipment vendors offer training to companies that lease or purchase their systems. Generally, the contract stipulates that the vendor will provide a certain amount of training to the purchaser's employees.

If you are chosen for vendor training, you can expect to be sent off-site to the vendor's facilities for training, or taught on your company's premises by a training representative of the vendor. In either case, training usually lasts for a relatively short period of time and must be supplemented by additional on-the-job training.

Like company training, vendor training is paid for by your employer, and you have the advantage of learning the system that you will be operating on a day-to-day basis.

Business School Training

The majority of business schools now offer courses in word processing in addition to their regular curricula. One advantage of these programs is that often they are relatively brief (one year or less) and can be enrolled in at varying times of the year.

Business schools also vary considerably in the size and quality of the word processing operation, reputation, and cost. You should personally visit any school that you are considering and talk to both students and administrators before signing a contract. When evaluating the word processing program at a business or secretarial school, make sure that the school is licensed by a state educational agency. This ensures that, at minimum, the school's operations meet basic state standards.

Training Through Temporary Help Services

In an effort to satisfy the overwhelming market demand for temporary word processing personnel, a number of temporary help services now conduct word processing training for qualified individuals. Those chosen for training are registered with the service, have an interest in word processing, and meet certain minimum requirements.

Applicants are closely screened before being accepted for WP training. Screening generally covers keyboarding, spelling, grammar, and communication skills. If you are accepted for training, you will learn one or more of the word processing systems that are available in the temporary service's offices. In many cases, hands-on equipment training will be coupled with some amount of conceptual training. Temporary help services do not charge a fee for word processing training. However, you must agree to work for the service for a certain minimum number of hours in exchange for your training.

Obtaining WP training from a temporary help service has a number of advantages. First, the training is free, except for your time commitment to the service. Second, jobs obtained through the service can get you the necessary experience and exposure to different types of businesses. In fact, some temporary WP employees have been asked to stay on permanently at businesses where they have proven their professionalism and willingness to work. Third, you often can be trained on more than one system, which makes you more marketable.

Other Sources of Training

Other training options do exist. You might investigate adult continuing education programs, technical schools, and vocational rehabilitation programs. Also, some local community groups now sponsor word processing seminars.

Finally, you always can teach yourself the fundamentals of word processing. If you have access to computer equipment and are willing to invest the time, it can be done. However, if the option is open to you, enroll in a formal program.

SELF-EVALUATION

Before committing yourself to a training program, take some time to do a complete self-assessment. In particular, seriously evaluate whether you have the personal attributes and technical skills that are necessary for a successful word processing career. These qualifications were discussed in detail in Chapter 4.

Personal Traits	*Technical Skills*
professionalism	typing skills
interest in word processing	interest in machines
dependability	English language skills
ability to handle pressure	ability to read, follow,
concentration	and interpret directions
human-relations skills	
task orientation	

A WP career is not for everyone. However, if you believe that you have what it takes, you are ready to become a part of the exciting field of word processing.

GAINING EXPERIENCE

Gaining hands-on word processing experience is an integral part of your individual training program. No matter how good your formal training program might be, you will need to get experience in order to sharpen your skills. Not only will experience make you a more efficient WP operator, it also will make you more marketable as you compete with other experienced operators for more interesting, higher paying WP positions.

There are a variety of ways to get experience, even while you are still training. You can apply for part-time positions and temporary jobs. Check your local newspaper, or register with a temporary service. You could hire yourself out as a freelance operator. There are many businesses and individuals willing to pay for one-time or short-term word processing help. You might even decide to volunteer your services to a worthwhile organization in exchange for machine time. Finally, if your school offers internships, you should try to get one.

The bottom line is that if you have experience, many more employment doors will be open to you.

CHAPTER 6

PRIMARY PLACES OF EMPLOYMENT

When considering a new career, it should have many opportunities for employment. Fortunately, a career in office automation fits these criteria. In every aspect of office automation, computer skills are in great demand. Because of that, your interest in other fields such as education, finance, or construction can be included with your word processing skills to secure a position that appeals to you.

Qualifications for word and data processing (DP) positions vary from one industry to the next and from one employer to the next. In general, entry-level WP and DP positions require, at a minimum, a high school diploma, keyboarding skills, and good command of the English language. Some companies are willing to provide training; others only will hire skilled equipment operators. In some fields, such as law and medicine, a working knowledge of the appropriate technical jargon may be required.

In this chapter, we will take a look at some of the major employers of word and data processing personnel. In particular, we will examine opportunities in the following fields: law, health care, the financial industry, government, large corporations, suppliers of temporary help, and the insurance industry.

Although far from complete, this list gives an idea of the range of employment opportunities available to you.

At the end of this chapter, you will find profiles of five individuals who work in the office automation field. Their experiences provide a realistic portrait of positions in several industries.

LAW

Many members of the legal profession enjoy the advantages offered by word processing systems. Users include sole practitioners; private law firms; federal, state, and local courts and agencies; corporate legal departments; and public interest groups.

Why does the legal profession find word processing so attractive? The practice of law is paper-intensive and deadline oriented, two characteristics that make it a prime candidate for word processing. Complex legal documents such as contracts, wills, legal briefs, leases, testimonies, and agreements are produced in staggering numbers, and they must be produced accurately and on schedule. Many of these documents go through a number of drafts on their way to final copy. The text-editing capabilities of word processing equipment make it possible to make revisions with speed and accuracy.

Although revisions are common, a significant amount of the language in legal documents is standard (or "boilerplate"). With word processing, key paragraphs and phrases that are used often can be stored and merged with variable text as needed.

Word processing also makes routine paperwork less tedious. Law offices report that they use their WP systems for correspondence, maintenance of docket-calendar control and client records, and billing.

Word processing opportunities in the legal field are plentiful. Today, most legal organizations use some type of word processing system. Equipment ranges from electronic typewriters to highly sophisticated shared and distributed logic systems. Word processing organizations range from one-person operations to large word processing departments. Some WP organizations work around-the-clock and even employ part-time workers as needed to share the heavy workload and maximize equipment efficiency.

Because of the demanding nature of legal work, employers are looking for highly skilled word processing operators, or trainable keyboarders, who can handle detail work and are willing to work long, hard hours. The rewards can be excellent. In general, the legal profession pays above-average salaries and is known for its excellent benefits.

HEALTH CARE

The health care profession also enjoys the benefits of word processing. WP systems can be found in many of the more than seven thousand hospitals and clinics in this country and in the offices of numerous doctors, dentists, and veterinarians in private practice. As health care costs continue to soar, word processing systems will become even more prevalent as individuals and organizations try to find ways to cut costs and become more competitive.

Word processors serve a variety of uses in the health care field. They are used to store and update patients' medical records; to handle appointments, billing, and insurance reports;

and to assist medical professionals in putting together reports, studies, and articles. Much routine correspondence (such as appointment reminders, introductions of new health care services, and fund-raising efforts) also can be handled efficiently with stored lists and common texts.

Word processing opportunities in the health care field are good. Positions require strong word processing skills and may require familiarity with medical terminology.

THE FINANCIAL INDUSTRY

Financial institutions, such as banks, credit unions, and finance and investment companies, vary considerably in the ways that they conduct their business affairs. However, one characteristic seems common to all: they are paper-intensive organizations that produce an abundance of written and numerical information. For most of these institutions, record keeping is automated and tends to be accomplished by large, computer-based systems that perform both word processing and data processing functions. Word processing is used to maintain detailed financial records; to produce newsletters, brochures, and training manuals; and to correspond with potential and actual customers.

Like many industries today, the financial industry is highly competitive. Word processing helps companies to attract and keep customers by providing them with excellent service. For example, word processing allows banks to automatically notify customers about the status of their savings and checking accounts and about new and improved services. In addition, word processing makes it possible to efficiently and economically send out mass mailings to attract new customers and to develop new sources of capital.

The financial industry is an exciting place for WP personnel. The industry relies heavily on sophisticated computer equipment and depends on skilled professionals to keep the systems up and running.

Many financial institutions have large word processing organizations that employ the full range of word processing personnel. Qualifications for word processing positions in the financial industry include good word processing skills; an interest in working with numbers; and accuracy, honesty, and discretion. Opportunities for advancement are excellent because of the industry's heavy reliance on office automation technology.

GOVERNMENT ORGANIZATIONS

Federal, state, and local government organizations are also major users of word processing systems. Because the range of services that these organizations provide is so vast, so are the word processing opportunities. A government word processing job might involve working in fields as diverse as personnel, law, health and welfare, education, housing, or transportation, among others.

In recent years, government organizations have become increasingly reliant on word processing systems. This is because WP helps them become more productive and cut costs, two major goals of all government bureaucracies.

In general, standard procedures exist for locating and applying for government jobs. At the federal level, contact your local federal job information center for information about WP employment opportunities and application procedures. At the state and local levels, government personnel agencies can point you in the right direction. If possible, use personal contacts such as friends and family members already employed by the government to find out about opportunities and to get a foot in the door.

Qualifications for government word processing positions vary. Generally, good keyboarding skills and adequate verbal and clerical aptitude can land you an entry-level position. Once you have entered the system, opportunities for advancement are very good. With the right amount of education and experience, you can advance to professional and administrative government positions.

LARGE CORPORATIONS

If you are interested in working for a large corporation, you will find that many word processing opportunities exist.

Today, word processing systems are found in practically all types of corporations. Manufacturers, marketing organizations, publishing companies, transportation firms, oil giants, and drug companies are just a few of the many industries that rely heavily on WP technology. These industries report using their systems for customer records and contacts, correspondence, billing, large mailings, customer service, public relations, corporate planning, reports, contracts, and financial records. And the list goes on and on.

Given the wide variety of WP applications used by businesses, it is not surprising that word processing systems often are found throughout the corporate organization. As a word processing employee, you might find yourself working in the personnel, legal, marketing, operations, customer service, or corporate planning department. Or you might find yourself on the team of a large, centralized word processing organization, performing a variety of word processing applications.

Corporate word processing opportunities are excellent. Virtually all large companies are committed to office automation as a means of improving worker productivity and increasing the speed and accuracy of operations. And word processing systems are a primary means of accomplishing these goals. Studies indicate that the majority of large corporations fill word processing vacancies primarily by training their own staff, and that most training takes place in-house. Therefore, if you are already employed by a company with word processing equipment and you are interested in learning the system, your chances of being trained by your employer are very good.

Spin-off career opportunities for corporate word processing personnel are also excellent. Many operators move on to supervisory WP positions and other computer-related positions, such as computer programmer, systems analyst, and equipment technician.

Many corporations pay above-average word processing salaries. When evaluating various companies, look at the size of the word processing operation, advancement potential, salary, benefits, and work environment to see if they meet your expectations.

TEMPORARY AGENCIES

Many businesses, at one time or another, require temporary help. Temporary services help companies meet their short-term word processing needs by providing them with temporary word processing employees. Temporaries fill in as vacation replacements, during peak workloads and rush jobs, and on onetime or short-term projects.

Whether you are an aspiring word processing operator or a skilled word processing professional, there are a number of reasons to consider registering with a temporary employment service. First, working at a variety of temporary jobs is an excellent way to gain valuable experience and to learn about different types of businesses. Second, temporary work gives you the option of saying no when you cannot or do not want to work. Most people with permanent jobs do not have this luxury. Third, temporary assignments can be taken while you are in-between jobs or on vacation from your regular work. For example, many teachers, college students, and others work as "temps" during their free time. Fourth, some temporary services provide word processing training to qualified individuals with an interest in the field. This can be a fast and inexpensive way to learn basic word processing skills. (See Chapter 5.)

The demand for temporary word processing employees is good. Temporary services are actively seeking experienced word processing professionals, newly trained WP operators, and WP trainees.

The financial rewards for temporary work are very good and increase with experience. On the average, temporary WP employees earn a higher hourly wage than temporary assistants, keyboarders, and other office support personnel.

THE INSURANCE INDUSTRY

Do you have an interest in the insurance industry? Word processors and other sophisticated automation systems are now standard equipment in most insurance companies, large and small. Without word processing, most of these companies could not survive in the highly competitive insurance market.

By their very nature, insurance companies produce tremendous quantities of information and paperwork. Word processors are used to store and update information on customer policies and claims and to maintain records of types of coverage available, associated premiums, and payment schedules. In addition, they are used to send out prospecting letters, billing notices, and notices of changes in coverage.

What kinds of word processing opportunities exist in the insurance industry? The number and variety of WP positions in the insurance industry are growing. WP personnel assist insurance agents and management-level personnel in handling their paperwork. Many larger insurance companies employ the full range of WP personnel to meet the tremendous workload. In addition, a growing number of insurance agents now have word processing equipment right at their desks to help them operate more efficiently. As an insurance agent, therefore, you might well be expected to operate word processing equipment on a day-to-day basis.

Good word processing skills and an interest in working with both numbers and people are prerequisites for a career in the insurance industry. Salaries and benefits vary considerably from one company to the next. Be sure to compare companies before taking a position.

INDIVIDUAL PROFILES

Angie Bigbee
Federal Government Assistant/Office Automation

Angie is an assistant who does most of her office work on the computer. She uses word processing, communication, database, and spreadsheet software to handle her job. Angie feels that she actually started in this career in middle school with her first typing classes. Throughout high school she continued taking office automation, shorthand, and bookkeeping courses. Then she joined the Army after high school and trained as a personnel management specialist, which in many respects is akin to being an assistant.

Every day at work Angie is confident that she uses the knowledge and skills that she acquired in school. She uses the office automation procedures and computer function keys and software that she learned in college. Angie believes that if you are really serious about a career in office automation, you need to make sure that your possess the following skills:

understanding of word processing, database, and spreadsheet programs

analytical skills

ability to enjoy putting information into a terminal

ability to work an eight-hour day seated in front of a computer monitor

good keyboarding skills

ability to follow directions

ability to concentrate in a room with other workers

ability to work with little supervision

ability to meet deadlines

Angie first used the computer when she was overseas with the Army, but she was using only word processing programs. However, after she left the Army she worked for the Army in family housing making assignments and keeping the budget. For this job, she used spreadsheets on the computer. Today Angie uses her personal computer on the job in many ways. She uses word processing software to write and format correspondence and to check for correct spelling and punctuation. She also uses a communication software package to download files from the mainframe computer through the local area network

(LAN). She uses database software to reformat the data and produce reports, and she keeps track of weekly production using a spreadsheet software package. Other duties include keeping track of expense items, distributing the many pieces of mail received in the office on a daily basis, ordering supplies, and keeping all files current.

Natalie Urich
Health Care Industry

Little Company of Mary Hospital is an acute care facility in southern California, run by the Sisters of the Little Company of Mary, a congregation of Catholic nuns. A variety of word processing equipment plays an important role in the day-to-day operations of the hospital. The medical records department, the pharmacy, and the health education department all use the equipment.

Natalie Urich is employed as administrative assistant to the hospital's director of development and community relations. Because her position requires her to produce a large volume and variety of paperwork, she was one of the first Little Company of Mary employees to be trained on the hospital's word processing equipment. Natalie readily admits that she was initially skeptical of the new equipment and its capabilities. Today, however, she has a word processor at her desk and relies on it for most of her daily output.

Natalie's primary responsibility is to support the director of development and community relations. One of the director's major responsibilities is hospital fund-raising. With the help of her word processor, Natalie produces fund-raising letters and other related materials. The hospital's mailing list is stored on disks, to be used selectively for various fund-raising efforts.

Word processing allows Natalie to personalize every letter that is sent out of the hospital without having to individually key each one. As Natalie explains, "The word processor saves time and results in a more professional-looking product. It helps present a much better image of the hospital."

Natalie highly recommends word processing training to anyone interested in an administrative career. She explains, "In hospitals and other businesses, the opportunities for an individual with a word processing background are endless."

Ronnie Stifter
Aerospace Industry

Ronnie Stifter is employed by an aerospace company in southern California. She is currently the supervisor of computer training. Her primary responsibility is coordinating the various in-house training programs that are offered to employees in her area. In particular, much of her work involves computer training of employees, including instruction on the use of word processing equipment and software.

As a training specialist for a large corporation, Ronnie has been able to combine two interests: teaching and computers. Prior to joining her present employer, she worked for thirteen years as a teacher at the preschool, kindergarten, and junior high school levels. Although she loved teaching, Ronnie decided to leave the profession to try her hand at something new and different. She found that opportunity in the aerospace industry.

During the last eight to ten years, Ronnie has held a number of positions. She worked for a while in finance and eventually became a computer programmer, after going back to school part-time and receiving a certificate in applications programming from UCLA.

While Ronnie was working as a programmer, a new word processing system was introduced. She was asked to learn the system and conduct a small amount of training. She did, and her training career "just naturally evolved" from that point on. As more office automation devices were added, more training was needed, and Ronnie often did it.

Ronnie believes that her teaching background has helped her to be a more effective corporate-level trainer. She points out that word processing, in particular, is one area where that background has been a real asset. "Just because you know word processing doesn't mean that you can teach it. . . . There's a skill to getting people to understand the system and to feel comfortable with it."

In her day-to-day work, Ronnie uses word processing, teaches it, and consults with other users who need her assistance. She particularly enjoys the consulting aspect of her work. She explains: "When you work with users, you have a much better idea of how they need to use the system, which means that sometimes we change our training program based on what we see people using it for. . . or what their needs are."

The users who work with Ronnie come from a variety of backgrounds. Some have a good deal of computer experience; others have none. Ronnie believes that the real keys to success in the word-processing field are a positive attitude and lots of hands-on experience. Those who keep an open mind and are willing to learn tend to be successful. And Ronnie believes that there is certainly no substitute for experience. "I think the only way to learn anything, whether you are going to be the trainer or not, is to use it. . . . You have to experiment, and if you are afraid to experiment, I think you lose a lot. At any training classes you go to, you are not going to learn everything there is to know about a system. You are going to get the groundwork so that you can leave and do basic things and go on from there. You are not going to be an expert. That is why on-the-job training and hands-on experience are so important."

What personal qualities does Ronnie think make for a successful word processing trainer? Lots of equipment experience and a true interest in teaching.

Violet Ridenour
Insurance Industry

Violet Ridenour began her training in data processing in a community college and received an associate degree in data processing. She then transferred to a four-year program at a university, where she is presently taking evening courses and will finish a degree in information science in another two years.

Between her junior and senior years, Violet applied for an internship in data processing and was accepted for training by Allstate Insurance Company. Her data processing courses from school gave her an advantage in completing the intensive assembler language training class. Upon the successful completion of the internship, she was hired by Allstate as an associate programmer. Her current position as programmer involves a variety of insurance applications.

At a giant insurance company, major users of systems products are divided into various divisions (for example, life systems, group systems, claims, marketing). Violet is working for life-health systems. Her job consists of coding new programs for any assigned projects, maintaining existing systems, and enhancing system designs. The work that she does helps the company keep track of clients' account balances, making sure all claims are paid and all payments are received.

At first, Violet found the change from school to a working environment a little difficult. The increase in responsibility that comes with manipulating live data for a large company, as opposed to school assignments, required some adjustment. In addition to this, a programmer may be called in after working hours if the system within her or his particular unit has aborted. Fortunately, in the year that she's been with the company, she's only been called once. After several months on the job, these new responsibilities have become a natural part of her job.

Violet works with people who maintain high standards of professionalism, while placing value on courtesy and friendship. She has learned to work as part of a team, in contrast to the individual approach that she experienced in school. When working as a team, communication, cooperation, timing, and even friendship become important.

The construction of a program involves both creativity and the exchange of ideas. The job has proved to be a tremendous learning experience for Violet. She has learned much about programming languages, different approaches to problem solving, and new programming strategies. She enjoys her job because it involves more than just the performance of daily routine. She sees each new project as a challenge. Having contributed to the completion of a successful project gives her a feeling of satisfaction and accomplishment.

Jeff Brandon
Computer Industry

Jeff Brandon is a systems programmer for McGraw Edison. His job is to maintain certain programs called systems software that help the company's entire data processing operation run. He is responsible for installing, testing, and implementing the operating system, the job entry subsystem that controls all input/output gear, the on-line compilers, and batch compilers.

Other primary responsibilities include supporting the security system software that prevents unauthorized access to computer files and the recovery management system for automatic restart of production jobs that have abnormally terminated. Jeff has secondary responsibilities for the company's teleprocessing environment, which includes the network control program and the telecommunications access method.

Another part of his job is assisting and training personnel. Applications programmers may need help in getting a program running or resolving a dump. Inexperienced personnel need special training that cannot be learned in a self-study course.

If a serious hardware problem exists, Jeff contacts the vendors to help resolve the problem. Other emergencies such as fires can occur where much of the data are lost or destroyed. The disaster recovery plan provides for backup files so that in case of a disaster, the company can begin functioning again in a relatively short time. Some tools Jeff utilizes to resolve problems and make changes in the software are manuals, terminals, and computer printouts.

Jeff really enjoys his job. He gets a personal satisfaction seeing something that he has worked on run on the computer, whether it be the entire operating system or a small portion of a single program.

Any testing that can't be done while other personnel use the system must be done on off hours, primarily evenings and weekends. Part of Jeff's job is working extra hours with little compensation, although if he needs time off, he usually gets it.

Jeff came into data processing as a computer operator trainee. Over the years, he worked his way through areas such as teleprocessing troubleshooting, performance tuning, operating procedure planning, JCL design, troubleshooting, and operations training. He received on-the-job training and was sent for specialized training offered by the company's vendors.

One thing Jeff can't stress enough for prospective programmers is that the job requires a lot of reading. The field of data processing changes too fast to sit down and memorize everything. One has to know which manual to look in to find the information desired. Jeff also has gained valuable guidance from working with more experienced systems programmers.

CHAPTER 7

RELATED OCCUPATIONS

There are many advantages to gaining the skills needed to work in the word processing profession. By acquiring the technical skills and experience needed to work in word processing, you are making yourself more appealing to employers in other fields. Becoming skilled as a word processor creates advantages that reach far beyond the realm of word processing and office automation.

There is a wide variety of spin-off careers that you might want to consider. Not surprisingly, many WP operators advance within the traditional word processing structure. They move on to positions as computer supervisors, managers, proofreaders, and trainers. Others find employment with computer equipment vendors in fields such as sales, marketing support, equipment service, and training. Less traditional spin-off possibilities include consulting, teaching, and operating your own home-based WP business.

When considering spin-off opportunities, it is important to keep in mind that word processing is just one aspect of office automation. Computers also serve a variety of other uses in businesses. Opportunities in the computer field are vast, and some word processing personnel naturally progress to these positions.

If you are interested in a more comprehensive look at computer careers, you may want to review the following books: *Opportunities in Computer Careers,* by Julie Kling Burns; *Careers in Computers,* by Lila B. Stair; and *Careers for Computer Buffs & Other Technological Types,* by Marjorie Eberts and Margaret Gisler.

Without a doubt, you will find many more career opportunities available to you as your level of education and work experience increase. However, if you are a relative newcomer to the word processing field with a limited amount of education, this should not deter you. With a high school diploma and technical word processing skills, it is still possible to spin off to other interesting positions.

Here are four suggestions for using your WP background to move on to new fields of endeavor:

- Try to switch careers within the company that presently employs you. This is your best bet for advancement. Internal promotions and lateral moves are common because many companies are willing to take a chance on employees who have already proven themselves in the business, even if their educational background and work experience are limited. If there are additional opportunities with your present employer, check them out.
- Use your professional contacts to find out about potential jobs. After working in the word processing field for a while, you will have developed a number of contacts (with principals within your own organization and vendor representatives, for example) who may be able to give you some job leads. Also, do not overlook the assistance of friends and acquaintances who work for other companies that interest you.
- Regularly scan employment ads that are placed in the local newspaper by businesses. The ads will give you an idea of

the types of jobs that are available and what qualifications you need to get them.

- Talk to employment agencies. Describe your background and aspirations. The agencies can give you valuable information about the current job market and how your credentials stack up in that market.

Before embarking on a new career, take the time to learn as much as you can about the field that interests you. If you are considering a career in computer programming, for example, go to your local library and read up on the subject. Talk to people who are already in that field. They can give you a realistic portrayal of what your day-to-day work would be like. If you have to go back to school for your new career, try to take one or two relevant courses while you are still at your present position to make sure that your interest is well-founded.

Most important of all, match yourself to the job. Determine which technical skills and personal attributes are necessary for the position that interests you, and make sure that you have what it takes.

In the rest of this chapter, we will be taking a look at some of the more popular spin-off careers for word processing personnel. These include:

- word processing supervision/management
- sales
- marketing support
- equipment service
- teaching
- computer programming
- systems analysis
- consulting
- home-based businesses

For each of these positions, we will discuss the nature of the job, qualifications, salaries, and the employment outlook.

MANAGEMENT

One of the most obvious and natural spin-off careers for word processing operators is WP management. As outlined in Chapter 3, word processing managers oversee the entire word processing operation of a company or of a WP division within a company. To recap, specific duties include developing procedures for word processing operations; selecting, directing, and guiding WP personnel; distributing the workload; maintaining liaison with upper-level management; and keeping up-to-date on new WP equipment and procedures. In addition, WP managers are often responsible for the division's budget, production reports, training schedules, and coordination of activities with the administrative side of the organization.

Many WP managers start out as word processing operators and gradually assume supervisory and management positions. Others are formally educated in management techniques and learn word processing on the job. If you are interested in eventually joining the WP management ranks, it would be to your advantage to get some formalized management training. Ideally, you should obtain a college degree, while concentrating on courses in management, human relations, communications, and word processing concepts and operations.

Because the position of WP manager is so demanding, employers are looking for individuals with word processing expertise, lots of hands-on experience, the ability to work well under pressure, a good educational background, excellent training and communications skills, and strong, well-developed interpersonal skills.

WP managers earn varied salaries depending on the size of the company and clerical staff, managerial responsibilities, and the complexity of the company's operations. WP managers earn between $21,500 and $38,900 depending on what part of the country they live in. Some WP managers go on to oversee a company's entire information processing operation. Others move on to management positions outside of the word/information processing field. Independent consulting is another viable and profitable option for the highly skilled WP manager.

SALES

Do you have an outgoing personality and strong communications skills? If so, you may be well suited for a career in computer equipment sales. Salespeople work for computer equipment vendors and are usually assigned a specific territory or industry to call upon. Their job is to assess a potential customer's computer needs and find a system that meets those needs. They then prepare a proposal for the customer that outlines the recommended system, its advantages, and associated costs. The salesperson's ultimate goal is to use his or her persuasive abilities to make a sale.

Qualifications for sales positions vary considerably. Although a college degree is generally not a prerequisite, it is becoming more and more common, especially in larger companies. Some companies require an associate degree or four-year degree in marketing or sales. Most vendors prefer that you have prior sales experience; it does not necessarily have to be in the word processing field, although some computer background is preferred. Once hired, sales representatives usually attend some formal or informal sales training classes that are intended to teach the vendor's specific approach to selling.

If you are interested in a career in sales, you should have excellent verbal and written communications skills, strong human relations skills, a sharp appearance, stamina, and self-confidence. Without a doubt, you should enjoy selling and be able to handle all of the pressures associated with such a demanding position.

Opportunities in sales are excellent. However, it is important to point out that competition among salespeople is fierce, and many individuals do not succeed in the field. If you are successful, a sales career can be very lucrative. Salaries are usually based on experience and individual performance. That is, you earn a base salary plus commissions on your sales. The median average salary for computer equipment salespeople is $36,100. In general, the middle 50 percent earn between $24,900 and $51,900. The bottom 10 percent earn less than $16,700, while the top 10 percent earn more than $75,000. Some salespeople may even earn in excess of $100,000 per year.

Along with their earnings, salespeople can be reimbursed for expenses such as entertaining customers, hotel and motel costs, and transportation costs. Some companies may offer incentive packages such as gifts or free vacation trips.

Advancement potential for members of the sales force is also excellent. Successful salespeople often join the management ranks of vendor companies because of their detailed knowledge of the market and the company's customer base.

MARKETING SUPPORT

Marketing support representatives (MSRs) also are employed by computer equipment vendors. The primary function of MSRs is to support the sales force. They do this by demonstrating the features and applications of equipment to new and potential customers, training new users on their systems, and consulting with customers about how they can better use their systems or how they can solve an equipment problem.

Many MSRs come from the ranks of word and data processing operators. Because of their own hands-on experience with WP and DP equipment, they are better able to understand customer needs and to effectively teach others how to use the system. Some MSRs have a teaching background and they apply those skills to their position. This, however, is usually not a prerequisite.

Some of the qualities that vendors look for in their MSRs include excellent communications skills, an understanding of people and their equipment problems and needs, teaching skills, persuasiveness, tactfulness, and diplomacy. Of course, a strong computer background is very important.

Many MSRs go on to careers in sales, and some move on to management positions in vendor organizations.

EQUIPMENT SERVICE

Equipment service representatives (ESRs) work for the repair or service departments of computer equipment vendors. The responsibilities of ESRs include installing new equipment at customer locations and servicing existing equipment. Servicing can involve routine preventive maintenance or emergency repairs. ESRs first become proficient at common repairs. Over time they may specialize in more difficult repair problems.

As you might well expect, ESRs have a background in electronics and equipment repair and are mechanically inclined. Although it is generally not a requirement, some ESRs have two- or four-year college degrees. Most employers of ESRs conduct their own training programs. Some have company repair schools. Other vendors conduct intensive on-the-job training. Because computer equipment is changing all the time, many ESRs attend brush-up classes and seminars on a regular basis to keep up-to-date about their equipment.

Because ESRs are the customer's primary connection with the vendor during installation and after training, they need to be quick and responsive to the customer's needs. The ability to handle pressure is essential, as ESRs are usually needed only when something has gone wrong with the equipment and the customer is losing valuable time and money. Other important traits would include initiative, organizational ability, interpersonal skills, and strong problem-solving ability.

A background as an equipment service representative eventually can lead to a career in sales, engineering, or even research and development.

TEACHING

Do you have experience in teaching or an interest in teaching? Computer instructors are increasingly in demand as the number of facilities that offer computer training continues to grow. Word processing instructors are needed in a variety of settings. Teaching positions are available at four-year and community colleges, private business schools, vendor companies, and private companies that conduct their own in-house WP training.

Many WP instructors have an A.A. or a B.A. in a field such as business education, business administration, or office occupations. Many also have teaching and/or word processing work experience.

WP instructors should enjoy teaching and working with people, have the ability to simplify seemingly complex material, and be thoroughly familiar with several word processing systems. In addition, they should have strong presentation skills and be patient and generous with their time.

The job outlook for word processing instructors is good. More and more schools are adding WP courses to their curricula, more businesses are investing in WP systems, and more vendors are offering WP training.

Salaries vary by region and industry.

COMPUTER PROGRAMMING

Computer programs are sets of instructions that tell a computer what to do. Computer programmers design computer programs and modify existing ones to better suit user needs. This involves taking a problem description (a routine that someone wants the computer to perform) and translating that description into a program written in computer language.

Many computer programmers begin their careers as trainees and gradually progress to more difficult assignments and higher-level programming positions. Many companies have programmer career ladders, offering opportunities for senior programmers, team leaders, and programming managers, among others.

Qualifications for computer programming positions are becoming more stringent all the time. Today, most companies require, at minimum, a bachelor's degree in a field such as data processing, computer science, accounting, or business administration. An associate degree in data processing or some course work in the field can still land you an entry-level position, but such opportunities are very limited. Some companies provide on-the-job training to qualified employees with little or no programming background. However, this is becoming much less common as the number of trained programmers in the work force continues to increase. In addition, there are numerous technical schools that offer computer programming courses. Colleges and technical schools, however, can now afford to be choosy. There are often many more applicants than spaces available because of the increased interest in the programming field.

What traits should a computer programmer possess? Successful programmers tend to have many of the following characteristics: creativity, problem-solving ability, a cooperative attitude, detail orientation, deadline orientation, the ability to handle stress, adaptability, neatness, orderliness, flexibility, the ability to work as part of a team, willingness to work long hours, and a logical mind.

Because computers are now standard business equipment, employment opportunities for computer programmers exist in practically every type of business. The United States Department of Labor, Bureau of Labor Statistics, reports:

> Employment of programmers is expected to grow much faster than the average for all occupations . . . as computer usage expands. . . . The need for programmers will increase as businesses, government, schools, and scientific organizations seek new applications for computers and improvements to the software already in use. Further automation of offices and factories, advances in health and medicine, and continuing scientific research will drive the growth of programmer employment.
>
> Employment, however, is not expected to grow as rapidly as in the past, as improved software and programming techniques simplify or eliminate some programming

tasks. The greater use of packaged software that can meet the needs of many users also may moderate the growth in demand for applications programmers.

Job prospects should be good for college graduates who are familiar with a variety of programming languages, particularly newer languages that apply to computer networking, data base management, and artificial intelligence.

On the average, computer programmers can earn between $30,700 and $52,000. College graduates with a bachelor's degree in the area of computer programming earn an average starting salary of about $35,167 in private industry, according to the National Association of Colleges and Employers.

Advancement potential for programmers is excellent. Many move on to positions as senior programmers, systems analysts, and data processing managers.

SYSTEMS ANALYSIS

Like programmers, systems analysts work closely with computers. Their job is to develop ways to improve the organization's use of its computer equipment. They do this by helping equipment users articulate their needs and by recommending ways that the computer system can meet those needs. In some instances, if the present equipment's capabilities are insufficient to solve a major problem, systems analysts may get involved in studying and recommending new equipment. Once a solution has been developed, they often work with the programming staff to implement the solution.

Because systems analysts work closely with equipment users, they must be highly informed about the different types of work that the company does. In addition, systems analysts must be well-versed in the capabilities of the company's computer system. They also should be aware of new technologies that are available to the company.

Systems analysts are generally considered to be a step above programmers on the career ladder. Therefore, they tend to have more experience and education than the average programmer. Today, a four-year college degree and some computer experience are the norm for most systems analyst positions, but graduate degrees are becoming more and more common. Courses in computer programming, word processing, data processing, and computer operations are helpful. Also, systems analysts should have a broad business background in order to understand the special needs and problems of system users.

Characteristics of successful systems analysts include the ability to think clearly and logically, strong written and verbal communications skills, analytical skills, the ability to work well with individuals from a variety of backgrounds, good business sense, and a background in computer programming (although this is not always required).

The job outlook for systems analysts is very good. The United States Department of Labor, Bureau of Labor Statistics, reports:

> Employment of systems analysts is expected to grow much faster than the average for all occupations. . . . College graduates who have had courses in computer programming, systems analysis, and other data processing areas as well as training or experience in an applied field should enjoy good prospects for employment. Persons without a college degree and college graduates unfamiliar with data processing will face keen competition from the large number of experienced workers seeking jobs as systems analysts.

Computer systems analysts earn impressive wages. Average annual earnings for systems analysts are $46,300. According to Robert Half International, Inc., starting salaries in 1997 for systems analysts ranged from $46,000 to $57,500. Salaries for those employed in small companies ranged from $38,000 to $48,000.

Advancement potential for systems analysts is also very good. Many go on to managerial positions in the data processing field or to other areas of the organization.

CONSULTING

Computer consultants are individuals who market their considerable computer expertise to businesses, often on a freelance basis. Consultants are hired by businesses for any number of reasons. They can provide knowledgeable advice about which system a company should install, how the equipment can best be utilized, and what types of training the company should invest in. Also, they are often employed to persuade upper-level management of the benefits of computers. In most cases, consultants are employed by a company only for a specified period of time or until a specific project is completed.

Consultants may work for a variety of industries, or they may specialize in a particular industrial field. Some work independently, while others are members of consulting groups or companies.

Qualifications for consultants include strong computer expertise, familiarity with a wide variety of equipment, creativity and objectivity, and a strong background in data processing and management. Although a degree is not as important as experience and knowledge, it certainly makes the consultant more marketable.

Experienced consultants can command excellent fees. At the present time, there is a real demand for their services.

HOME-BASED WORD PROCESSING BUSINESSES

Do you enjoy your independence? Would you like to be self-employed? If so, you will not want to overlook the possibility of using your computer skills to start your own home-based WP business. In ever-increasing numbers, skilled WP operators with business know-how are choosing to leave the traditional job market and open up their own home-based word processing operations. Their clients include companies with an overflow of work; companies without word processing equipment; students, professors, and writers with papers to be typed; and small businesses with little or no support staff.

To open up shop, you need to have the following: equipment that is sophisticated enough to meet your clients' needs, top-notch skills, marketing skills to market yourself and your service, and business contacts. Good business sense will come in handy for determining fees and handling clients on a professional basis. In addition, you need to have drive, ambition, management skills, and a commitment to your business.

There are many advantages to working for yourself. First and foremost, you get to be your own boss. You do not have to answer to anyone but yourself and your clients. You can set your own hours and work at your own speed. You can chart your own future. If you want your business to stay small, it can. If you want to expand your operations, the sky can be the limit.

Potential disadvantages also should be considered. As a self-employed worker, you do not get paid vacations or the other benefits associated with traditional jobs. Also, you must attract regular business or you do not get paid. If your marketing skills are weak, you become ill, or your clients no longer need your services, your business will probably not survive.

Salary potential as a self-employed worker depends on how much or how little you want to work. Even on a part-time basis, home-based word processing can be very lucrative.

CHAPTER 8

TODAY'S AUTOMATED OFFICE

Fortunately, "the office of the future" is here today for many businesses and soon will be available for most others. Many offices today rely on the technological innovations of office automation to ensure increased productivity and creativity. To compete with other businesses, these automated systems have become indispensable to businesses of all sizes.

Current office automation (OA) systems have proven very effective in increasing worker productivity and containing office costs, two critical business goals. Given these results, it is not surprising that most businesses support additional research and development in the OA field. This wholehearted commitment to OA by the business community provides manufacturers with the impetus they need to improve on current technology.

As a result, substantial progress continues to be made in the OA field. Exciting innovations are being developed and marketed all the time. And just as quickly as new developments are introduced, even more astonishing advances are announced.

In the word processing field alone, many improvements continue to be made to current systems to make them more efficient as well as more compatible with other OA technology. In fact, word processing and other OA equipment take a "systems approach" to the workplace. Manufacturers have developed

111

automated tools that work in harmony, not at odds, with one another. Today, businesses can purchase OA packages, instead of having to buy many individual and often incompatible pieces of automated equipment. These OA packages are designed to meet the many and varied computer needs of companies, including word processing.

Not too long ago, many people predicted that OA would eventually result in the elimination of most office jobs. Although growth in the field has slowed down in the past few years, word processing and other automated systems continue to create many interesting and new career options for office workers. As we have seen, a variety of opportunities abound in all types of organizations; and because of the dynamic nature of the OA field, additional opportunities will continue to unfold.

As an aspiring OA professional, you should be familiar with the latest trends and opportunities in computers and office automation. Why? Such knowledge will help you to better clarify your own career goals and will make you a more informed business professional. In the remainder of this chapter, we will take a brief look at some of the exciting advances that have been made in word processing and OA technology recently. In addition, we will see what impact those advances are having on business organizational patterns and employment opportunities in the OA field.

MULTIFUNCTION WORKSTATIONS

Although our discussion of WP systems has primarily centered on the single-purpose word processor with monitor, you should note that because this machine is capable of performing only WP tasks, the business community is increasingly turning toward using multifunction workstations. These workstations are equipped with computers that generally contain various software programs that will allow the user to accomplish a variety of WP tasks. In addition, they are often linked to the company's network, which can allow the user to communicate with coworkers via E-mail and share documents on a network drive.

Because of the versatility of these workstations, word processing departments in larger organizations and administrative assistants who handle the WP functions for smaller companies have found their day-to-day activities altered. Their responsibilities may be increased because of their abilities to handle both word processing and data processing tasks. Or, whole departments and assistants may find their skills are no longer needed and their workload is distributed throughout the organization. In any event, there always will be a need for the competent worker who is well versed in word processing.

COMMUNICATING TERMINALS

Many word processing and multifunctional terminals at different locations are capable of communicating with one another. Communication is accomplished by the transmission of data at high speeds by electronic means, usually using telephone lines or satellites. The equipment user keys information into a terminal in one location and, with the push of a button, sends it to a communicating terminal at another location. The receiving terminal stores the data and is able to print them out. All of these activities occur almost instantaneously.

With this technology, transmissions can occur over any distance—within an office building, within the same city, or between offices hundreds of miles apart. In the word processing field, this communications capability is often used to "share" work and data among operators or principals who are spread out at two or more locations.

A growing number of WP and multifunctional terminals are also electronically linked to the company's central computer system or network. In other words, individual terminals can communicate with the main computer. This permits terminal users to access the company's central data bank and, in some instances, to share the main computer's logic and storage power. With this capability, individual managers have access to computerized information as diverse as inventory records, personnel data, and sales forecasts.

Many terminals also have access to sources of data outside of the company. For a fee, terminals can communicate with external data banks, which offer such specialized information as stock market reports, general news, legal decisions, and much more. Use of these external information sources by businesses is on the rise because user fees are declining and more terminals are becoming capable of accessing these data banks.

E-MAIL

No longer is it always necessary to send mail by way of the post office or to have it hand-delivered by a messenger. Today, you can send messages to other people by means of electronic signals rather than paper and ink.

In-house E-mail systems are in place in most businesses. These systems make it possible for employees to exchange messages with one another. How do these systems work? The messages are transmitted electronically using a network of interconnected communicating terminals. In traditional offices, employees have wooden, plastic, or metal in-baskets on their desks for receiving incoming mail and messages. In companies with E-mail systems, employees have electronic in-baskets, which list all messages that have arrived at their terminal. At the touch of a button, the messages appear on the monitor. After each message has been read, it can be deleted from the system, filed for future reference, returned to the sender with a reply, or routed to another employee.

Internal E-mail systems allow all of the members of an organization to be more productive. A significant amount of time is saved because employees no longer play "telephone tag," exchanging calls back and forth as they try to reach one another by telephone. In addition, E-mail systems reduce paperwork, thus allowing workers to be more efficient and more productive.

Today, with the push of a button, it is possible to quickly and effortlessly send messages, or "mail," electronically to people around the world. Privacy is maintained with message retrieval via a password.

OPTICAL CHARACTER READERS

An optical character reader (OCR) is a piece of equipment that scans text that has been typed on a standard typewriter and converts the characters in that text into electronic signals that can be recorded onto magnetic disks or tapes. In essence, an OCR automatically converts a typewritten document into a form useable by a word processor, eliminating the need to have an equipment operator key the original document into the WP system.

For example, suppose you have just typed a three-page document on an electric typewriter. Now you realize that a lot of revisions are going to have to be made, and it would be very helpful to have the document on a word processor. With an OCR, it is possible to scan the typewritten copy and record it on disks. This eliminates the tedious task of retyping the document into a form acceptable to the word processor.

For many companies, investment in an optical character reader is very attractive. With an OCR, a company can continue to use standard office typewriters as the first step in the word processing cycle. Documents are typed on the typewriter, scanned by the OCR, then edited and formatted on WP equipment. With this capability, businesses can obtain the efficiencies of word processing, while investing in fewer costly WP systems.

VOICE-ACTIVATED WORD PROCESSING

The most time-consuming aspect of word processing is keying the original document into the WP system. The day is coming, however, when the keyboarding task may be obsolete. Because voice-recognition technology is progressing so rapidly, it is realistic to predict that keyboards eventually will become a thing of the past and voice-activated word processing equipment will become commonplace.

In time, you will be able to "speak" to your computer and have your words accurately converted into text on the WP screen. In fact, equipment capable of distinguishing words already exists. Much more research is needed, however, before such equipment becomes a practical reality. Machines would have to be able to understand a variety of speech patterns and accurately spell and punctuate before they could be widely used. Nevertheless, voice-recognition experts predict that day is near.

LAPTOPS

The trend in computer hardware development is toward more compact, multifunctional equipment. One manifestation of this trend is the laptop, a lightweight system that is small enough to fit inside a briefcase. Its small size enables people who must travel a great deal to carry their computer with them and use it outside of the traditional office setting.

Two of the most frequent uses served by portable computers are word processing and communications. With laptops, users can produce letters, memos, and other documents with ease. Then, using the communications capability of the laptop equipment, the documents can be sent electronically, usually by means of telephone lines, to distant locations. This feature makes it possible for businesspeople who are on the road to keep in touch with the home office, customers, and the company database, even though they may be separated from one another by many miles. For example, the portable computer can be used by the traveling executive to communicate with customers and members of the company staff. In addition, that same computer may provide the executive with corporate sales data, price lists, and even personal messages from the home office.

PERSONAL COMPUTERS IN THE HOME

As we have entered the twenty-first century, multifunctional computers with word processing capabilities are commonplace in most households. In fact, personal computer systems (also referred to as home computer systems), ranging in price from several hundred to several thousand dollars, are in place and serving a variety of uses in millions of homes. Typically, home computers are used to play electronic games, balance the checkbook, and do simple word processing. However, more and more families also are using their systems for many of the same applications as businesses do, including detailed financial record keeping, list maintenance, sophisticated word processing, and business transactions, such as banking and bill paying.

Today, more families depend on home computers to handle most of their day-to-day business, including bookkeeping, budgeting, bill paying, and all financial record keeping. Those same computers also are used to maintain detailed lists of everything from phone numbers to birthdates, and to maintain inventories of household items such as books, magazines, tools, and even recipes.

Elementary schools and high schools have also introduced students to computers in the classroom. Computers are increasingly becoming standard teaching aids, making the three Rs easier and more fun for students to learn. And as increasing numbers of children learn about and come to rely on computer technology, computers will find their way into even more and more homes.

Home computers with communications capabilities already give consumers access to a wide variety of external data, such as stock market reports, weather information, and sports data. Every type of information imaginable is available to home computer owners in seconds. In addition, families can send most of their business and personal mail by computer and communicate electronically with people around the world.

These are only a few of the many exciting present applications of home computers.

DESKTOP PUBLISHING

Desktop publishing is the process of producing newsletters, magazines, and even books with a personal computer. It goes beyond word processing, in that it allows the user to manipulate the layout of the document and mix graphics with text. With a personal computer, a desktop publishing program, and a laser printer, it is possible to quickly and easily produce documents that once required the skills of a typesetter, an art department, and a professional printing press.

THE INTERNET

The term "Internet" stands for "interconnected networks." It is the world's largest computer network, linking smaller computer networks worldwide. Using phone or cable lines, the Internet links personal computers and mainframes around the globe. This makes it possible for computer users to access a vast array of information.

For example, through the Internet you can access such diverse data as the U.S. Census Bureau's files, airline schedules, and satellite weather maps. You can send and receive messages using your own personal E-mail. You even can access up-to-the-minute news and stock market data.

There are a number of ways to access the Internet. Commercial on-line services offer Internet access, charging a fee for on-line time. As more and more businesses and individuals access the Internet and become aware of its enormous capabilities, the manner in which information is gathered and processed will continue to change, resulting in even greater efficiencies.

ORGANIZATIONAL TRENDS

As described in Chapter 3, the three most common organizational patterns that result when businesses implement word processing systems are centralized word processing, decentralized word processing, and word processing adapted to the traditional office structure. In the 1960s and 1970s, centralized word processing structures were undoubtedly the most popular. When businesses first invested in WP, many decided to establish separate word processing and administrative support centers to provide specialized support to the organization. As a result, word processing equipment was put in a central location and was operated only by the word processing staff.

In the 1980s and 1990s, businesses moved toward a systems approach to the workplace and the growth of low-cost, multi-functional computer equipment. With this change, some of these businesses have begun to reassess their centralized word processing structures. Instead of isolating equipment in a central location, many businesses chose to place automated equipment throughout the office, where it can be used by assistants, managers, technical writers, analysts, clerks, and anyone else who needs to access and process information. These days a computer at one's workstation is often commonplace.

Even though many businesses continue to move away from a totally centralized approach to word processing, most of them still hire full-time WP operators and other WP professionals to carry out and oversee large and complicated word processing tasks. These WP personnel often work closely with other equipment users in the organization to ensure the effective use of the WP system.

EMPLOYMENT TRENDS

What impact will all of these developments have on employment opportunities for word and data processing professionals? Because of their technical expertise, WP and DP personnel will continue to enjoy a real advantage in the job market for many years to come. As employers continue to integrate newer and more sophisticated equipment into their office automation systems, they will be looking for professionals who already have experience in an automated environment. Individuals with word and data processing skills will be in demand, and they will have many flexible career options available to them.

New positions for individuals with word and data processing backgrounds continue to unfold. Consultants, systems analysts and designers, equipment operators and technicians, trainers, supervisors, and more are needed in virtually every industry. Jobs that once were considered clerical, such as equipment operator, are becoming technical specialties. They generally require more education, but the payback comes in the form of higher salaries and more opportunities for advancement. The greatest long-term opportunities exist for individuals who are well versed in several aspects of OA technology, such as WP, data processing, and E-mail systems.

In sum, the word and data processing and office automation fields will continue to offer many diverse and interesting career choices for years to come, and those careers will pay above-average salaries, offer challenges, and provide a strong foundation for professional growth and development.

CHAPTER 9

PLANNING A CAREER IN TODAY'S AUTOMATED OFFICE

By this point, you probably have a good idea of whether a career in word/data processing is right for you. This will turn out to be one of the most important decisions you'll ever make, and you should make it carefully. Many people don't take the time to properly assess their skills and interests and subsequently find themselves locked in a field they would rather not be in. Reading this book is your first step to avoid that pitfall. The information given here will place you on the path to a rewarding and exciting future in office automation.

This chapter offers some basic guidelines for career planning and job hunting. If you desire additional information or assistance, you should consult your local library. A number of excellent books provide step-by-step career guidance. For example, *What Color Is Your Parachute? A Practical Manual for Job-Hunters and Career Changers,* by Richard Nelson Bolles, is a widely acclaimed career planning guide, and there are many others.

YOUR CAREER GOALS

Before you start applying for positions, it is important that you clarify your personal career goals. It is not enough to say that you want to be a word processing operator or an equipment technician. Your goals should be based on a clear understanding of your individual characteristics and how they match up with the job market that interests you. Once you have a good understanding of yourself, you will find it much easier to obtain a satisfying position in the job market.

Conducting a Personal Inventory

To gain a better understanding of the types of work you may qualify for and enjoy, you should conduct a complete analysis of your interests, abilities, skills, and past accomplishments. Some of the questions you may want to consider include:

- What types of work do you enjoy doing? What types of work do you dislike? For example, do you like or dislike keyboarding, filing, public speaking, managing people, managing projects, writing, working with equipment? Be specific.
- Do you have any special skills or abilities that you enjoy using? For example, are you good at understanding technical equipment?
- Do you enjoy working closely with other people, or do you prefer to work by yourself?
- Are you looking for a long-term career opportunity or a temporary position? Are you interested in a career with growth potential?

- Do you enjoy responsibility? Are you looking for a position with responsibility?
- How well do you handle pressure? Do you want a position that involves a lot of pressure?
- What aspects of past jobs did you like or dislike?
- How do you rate your communications skills? Do you enjoy writing or speaking in public?
- What is your educational background?

By studying your answers to questions such as these, you should begin to develop a better understanding of the kinds of work you should or should not consider. For example, a position as a WP or DP equipment operator is probably not for you if you do not especially enjoy keyboarding and do not like being confined to one area for long periods of time. On the other hand, if you like people, have an outgoing personality, and have strong communications skills, you should consider the possibility of a career in computer training, sales, or marketing support.

Exploring Career Options in Office Automation

After taking your personal inventory, you should explore career options in the field that interests you. As an aspiring OA professional, you will want to investigate all potential job options in the word processing field. Your research should result in a list of various types of OA positions, the responsibilities associated with each, skill requirements, educational requirements, working conditions, salary ranges, and opportunities for growth and advancement.

This information can be gathered from a number of different sources. In addition to this book, there are several good OA reference sources available. The Bibliography at the end of this book provides a list of some of those reference materials. Also, you should spend time talking to people who are already employed in the OA field. Informational interviews with WP and DP personnel can give you a much better idea of what specific jobs are really like. Finally, you may want to get in touch with professional associations, such as the International Association of Administrative Professionals. In general, such organizations can provide you with career information and may even have information about possible WP positions in your area.

Establishing Your Career Goals

Once you have taken a personal inventory and have explored possible career options, it is time to establish your career goals. Specifically, the kinds of questions you will want to consider include:

- What types of positions interest you?
- Do you have the necessary personal traits and technical skills for those positions?
- Are you willing to return to school to develop or upgrade your skills?
- What salary do you require?
- What salary do you expect?
- In what locality do you want to find employment?
- What type of company do you want to work for? Are you interested in any particular industry? Do you prefer a large or small organization?
- What kind of office environment do you prefer? Centralized? Decentralized? A combination of the two?
- Are you looking for full- or part-time work?

- What hours can you work?
- Are you interested in responsibility and growth potential?

The result of this process should be a clearly stated career goal. For example, your goal might be to obtain a permanent, full-time position as an entry-level word processing operator, making at least $24,000 per year, working for a law firm in Cleveland. Your long-term goal might be to attain the position of WP manager in that or a similar business within a five-year period.

BECOMING QUALIFIED

Once you have clearly outlined your career goals, you need to develop a strategy for achieving those goals. If you already have the educational background and skills required for the position that interests you, you can start investigating potential employers. However, if you are not yet qualified, you will need to take steps to remedy the situation.

Ask yourself the following questions: What are the minimum educational requirements and skills necessary for the position that interests me? How can I meet those requirements? (Chapter 5 describes OA training.) If you have the time and money, you should seriously consider returning to a classroom environment to obtain the necessary training. If you cannot afford full-time training, it is still possible to acquire skills. Find out whether your present employer offers in-house training opportunities or if the company will pay for you to attend school on a part-time basis. In addition, investigate financial aid opportunities at schools that you are interested in attending. Today, most schools offer financial assistance in the form of scholarships, grants, and loans. Information can be obtained directly from the schools' financial aid offices.

Finally, while training for a career in OA, try to get as much hands-on work experience, paid or volunteer, as you can. Experience will sharpen your skills and will make you more marketable when you begin looking for a job.

INVESTIGATING PROSPECTIVE EMPLOYERS

Because they are anxious to put their newly acquired skills to work, many people take the first job that they are offered. Do not fall into this trap. Keep in mind that finding the right employer probably will involve considerable time and research. Therefore, do not be easily discouraged. Your commitment of time and energy will undoubtedly pay off in a rewarding word processing position.

Where should you look for prospective employers? The following list represents some of the more common sources of word processing employment. If possible, explore them all. In addition, be creative. Use your imagination, and the right position will eventually materialize.

Your present company.   Do you enjoy working for your present employer? If so, investigate word processing employment opportunities right in your own office. Find out about company-sponsored training programs. Many companies have their own in-house training programs or pay for employees to be trained outside of the company. If these opportunities exist, make sure that you let the right people know that you are interested and want to be considered. In addition, discuss the opportunities for growth and advancement with your supervisor. There may be no need for you to extend your job search any further than your present place of employment.

School placement offices.   Some employers list available job openings with school placement offices. They do so because of the excellent reputations associated with the graduates of particular schools. If you are currently enrolled at a school that offers computer training and has a placement office, be sure to take advantage of this excellent job source.

Help-wanted advertisements.   One of the easiest ways to find out about employment opportunities in your community is to read the daily and Sunday classified sections of the local newspaper. The ads can be a valuable source of information about which companies are hiring, what positions are available, the nature of particular jobs, types of equipment skills in demand, experience requirements, and salary levels.

Help-wanted ads also are placed in magazines and newspapers associated with particular industries. If, for example, you are interested in a WP position in the advertising field, you should take a look at advertising trade journals.

Employment services.   The main goal of employment agencies and temporary help services is to match employers with employees. Employment agencies fill permanent positions while temporary services fill temporary job openings. Both types of employment services fill word processing positions for employers and should not be overlooked as a job source. In fact, a growing number of services specialize in word processing job placement. These services have developed working relationships with a number of local companies and fill many of their positions. If you do become involved with an employment service, make sure that you understand any fee arrangements before you sign a contract.

Your public library.   Your local public library can provide a wealth of information about prospective employers in your community as well as throughout the country. Business and other directories offer detailed information about a wide variety of companies and industries. Most libraries also can provide you with lists of business and professional organizations, trade associations, and community organizations that are relevant to your field of interest. The reference librarian can assist you in gathering this information.

Government employment offices.   Federal, state, and local government organizations are major employers of computer personnel. Government employment offices or job information centers maintain lists of all currently available positions and the specific requirements for those positions. In most instances, there are standard procedures for applying for these jobs and deadlines for filing applications. You can obtain this information directly from the employment offices.

Word of mouth.   Using personal contacts, or "networking," can be one of the most effective ways of finding out about job openings and getting a foot in the door. Therefore, you should let as many people as possible know that you are looking for a job and describe your interests. This means family, friends, former employers, and anyone else who may have information about job openings.

The phone book.   Your phone book can serve as a business directory. If you are interested in working for a particular type of business or industry, it makes sense to look in the yellow pages of your phone book for a list of all companies in your area in that line of work.

Gathering details about prospective employers is no easy task. If possible, the information that you amass about each should include the following: a company profile, types of positions available, position descriptions, necessary qualifications, salaries and other benefits, computer systems used, opportunities for advancement, and working conditions. With all of this information at your fingertips, you then can make an intelligent decision about which employers you are interested in approaching.

PREPARING A RESUME AND COVER LETTER

In many instances, your first contact with a prospective employer will be by mail. It is therefore important that you prepare a cover letter and resume that will make a favorable first impression and get you an interview.

The cover letter that accompanies your resume serves a number of important functions. It briefly introduces you to the prospective employer, expresses your interest in a particular position, mentions your qualifications for the job, and explains why you want to work for that particular company. Your cover letter should be brief, but interesting and informative. And, like your resume, it should be error free.

The resume itself should be an accurate, interesting, and attractive presentation of your background, skills, and abilities. There are many different theories as to how a resume should be organized and the types of information it should include. You will want to put your name, address, and phone number at the very top. For a word processing position, for example, you will need to list all word processing training and other relevant education. Also, you will need to point out all relevant work experience—paid or volunteer. You also may want to include type of work sought, honors and offices, memberships in professional associations, and references. (Most resumes end with "References available on request" or a similar phrase.)

If you are just entering the job market you will want to stress your relevant training and educational background. If you are already employed in the OA field, emphasize both your experience and training.

The way that all this information is organized is largely a matter of personal taste and preference. There are two basic resume styles. The chronological resume lists your work experience in chronological order, beginning with your most recent job. The functional resume expresses your qualifications in categories, such as sales and management skills. It emphasizes job functions instead of dates of employment. Numerous books have been written on the resume writing process, including *How to Write a Winning Resume,* by Deborah Perlmutter Bloch, and *Resumes Made Easy,* by Patty Marler and Bailey Mattia, both published by VGM Career Books. You should refer to several of them before making a final determination.

Sometimes you will need to go directly to a company's employment office and fill out one of their standard applications before being considered for a position. If this is the case, be sure to bring all relevant information with you, including the names and phone numbers of references, and any other important names and dates. When filling out the application, be neat and thorough. The application, like your resume, is a reflection of you.

INTERVIEWING

The job interview is the next step in the job-hunting process. This step often terrifies interviewees, as it can make or break the job offer. The best way to overcome your fears is to be prepared for the interview and to keep in mind that you have a skill that is needed by the interviewer's company.

Before you go to the interview, find out as much as possible about your prospective employer and the job for which you are applying. Make a list of any questions you have, and do try to have some. If you do not know the salary being offered for the position, have a particular salary range in mind. Review your background and qualifications, and be prepared to discuss them in detail. In addition, take into consideration these recommendations by the U.S. Department of Labor:

- Dress appropriately.
- Show interest and enthusiasm for the job and the company. A good attitude is often as important as your actual qualifications for the job.
- Prepare ahead of time for difficult questions. These might include: Tell me about yourself? Where do you want to be five or ten years from now? What are your major strengths and weaknesses? What special contribution can you make to our organization? What kind of salary are you looking for? Why are you interested in a word or data processing position? How long do you plan to work for our organization?

Many career planning books offer valuable advice about the interviewing process, including how to handle such tough questions. You would be wise to spend some time reading and preparing for the job interview. Some VGM Career Books to review include *How to Have a Winning Job Interview,* by Deborah

Perlmutter Block, and *Job Interviewing for College Students,* by John D. Shingleton.

AFTER THE INTERVIEW

After every interview, be sure to thank the interviewer for his or her time, and remember to send a follow-up thank you letter. A short note of thanks often makes a lasting and favorable impression and provides you with one more chance to express your interest in the job.

CHOOSING THE RIGHT JOB

The result of all of this hard work probably will be one or more job offers from companies that interest you. In the final analysis, only *you* can decide which job offer is right for you. Before you make a decision, be sure to review all the facts about each position, and review your personal goals. If you are lucky, the choice will be clear!

CONTINUING TO PLAN YOUR CAREER

The fact that you are reading this book indicates your interest in planning for your future. It is important to keep in mind that career planning does not end once you find suitable employment. Indeed, it is a process that should continue throughout your professional life.

As an office automation professional, there are a number of things that you should continue to do throughout your career. Read, take additional courses, attend trade shows and seminars, join professional associations, and develop and maintain professional contacts. By doing so, you will be helping to ensure yourself a satisfying and rewarding future in the office automation field.

PROFESSIONAL ORGANIZATION

International Association of Administrative Professionals
10502 Northwest Ambassador Drive
P.O. Box 20404
Kansas City, MO 64195-0404

As the world's leading association for administrative staff, the International Association of Administrative Professionals (IAAP) promotes excellence through continuing education, leadership training, publications, international networking, access to research findings, and more.

IAAP has nearly forty thousand members and affiliates and 640 chapters worldwide. Its members include administrative assistants, executive assistants, office supervisors, information specialists, and other administrative professionals. Corporate executives, business educators, trainers, and students also are involved as members.

"IAAP provides information and resources to help administrative professionals contribute more effectively to their organizations," said Candy Daniels, CPS, of Ruston, Louisiana, 2000–2001 international president of IAAP. Major services offered by the Kansas City, Missouri–based IAAP include:

Education and training. IAAP and its local chapters host a variety of seminars, workshops, and conferences featuring internationally recognized speakers. IAAP's largest training event is its International Convention and Education Forum held each summer. In addition, the headquarters office offers member discounts on more than 250 books, self-study workbooks, and videotapes on all facets of office administration, many with the continuing education unit (CEU).

Networking. Members build professional networks by attending chapter meetings and serving in chapter leadership positions. Members also can serve as division, district, and international officers. The association's website (www.iaap-hq.org) also allows for on-line international networking.

Professional certification. Certification from IAAP is an internationally recognized standard of excellence. IAAP currently offers the Certified Professional Secretary (CPS) rating, and starting in May 2001 will introduce the Certified Administrative Professional (CAP) program covering an expanded scope of administrative skill and knowledge. To achieve certification, the candidate must pass an intensive exam encompassing finance, business law, office technology, communications, behavioral science in business, and so forth. More than fifty-eight thousand office professionals have achieved the CPS rating.

Research. IAAP monitors current trends and practices in the administrative profession and is a clearinghouse for information and research findings.

OfficePRO magazine. IAAP's award-winning magazine offers readers a wealth of tips and advice on career development and office administration.

Administrative professionals week.   IAAP first organized and is the sole official sponsor of Administrative Professionals Week (formerly Professional Secretaries Week), conducted annually during the last full week in April since 1952. The observance recognizes the contributions of administrative professionals and is used by many IAAP chapters as a time for professional development events.

For further information on IAAP professional development programs and services, call (816) 891–6600 or visit IAAP's website at www.iaap-hq.org.

GLOSSARY

Blind Word Processing System—A word processing system that does not have a monitor.

Block Movement—A WP feature that makes it possible for a WP operator to define a block of text by marking its beginning and end with the cursor, and then to manipulate the entire block at once. For example, using this feature, a block of text can be moved to a new location in the text, deleted, or duplicated.

Boilerplate Data—Key paragraphs and phrases that are used over and over again in one or several documents.

CD-ROM—A disk resembling an audio compact disc that retains files and programs. Stands for "compact disk–read only memory."

Centering, Automatic—A WP feature that makes it possible to center a word, line, page, or even an entire document, if desired, automatically.

Central Processing Unit (CPU)—The internal part of the WP equipment that is responsible for processing, storing, and retrieving data from memory. It is often called the *microprocessor,* or *computer's brain.*

Centralized Word Processing—A word processing organizational structure that involves concentrating WP equipment in a central location that services multiple departments or groups within the organization.

Command Keys—Special keys on the WP keyboard that enable the WP operator to give the machine instructions, such as delete, insert, move text, store, search, and print.

Cursor—A small character of light on the monitor that shows where the next character typed by the operator will appear. As the operator keys text into the word processor, the cursor moves across the screen to help the operator keep his or her place.

Database—A large source of information that can be referred to in many ways.

Decentralized Word Processing—A word processing organizational structure in which smaller clusters of word processing equipment take the place of large, centralized WP pools.

Delete—A WP feature that allows you to delete, or erase, characters, words, phrases, paragraphs, or even larger blocks of text.

Display Word Processing System—A word processing system that is equipped with a monitor.

Distributed Logic System—A category of word processing equipment in which several WP terminals share computer power, storage, and printers and can communicate with one another. Individual terminals have some intelligence of their own.

Editing Functions—Special WP functions that make it possible for text to be keyed into the system and then revised without having to rekey the entire document. Typical editing functions include insert, delete, block moves, and search.

Electronic Typewriter—A low-level word processor that contains a microprocessor, limited memory, and some additional keys that make it possible to perform basic editing and formatting functions.

Ergonomics—The application of biological and engineering data to problems pertaining to people and machines.

External Storage Devices—Mechanisms that permanently record and store information keyed into the word processing system.

Typical external storage devices include floppy disks, Zip disks, and CD-ROMs.

File—A set of related information that is stored as a unit on an external storage device.

Floppy Disk—A small, removable disk that contains any stored information.

Formatting Functions—Special WP functions that make it possible to alter the physical appearance of a document, including width of margins, line length, and page length.

Global Search and Replace—A WP feature that makes it possible to search for a word, phrase, or sentence in a document and replace it with another.

Hard Copy—Readable copy printed on paper, as opposed to information still stored in the computer and displayed on a monitor.

Headings and Footings—Repetitive words or phrases that appear at the top and/or bottom of each printed page of a document. The automatic heading/footing feature makes it possible to key the repetitive words only once and then have the word processor automatically print them on each page.

Hyphenation—A WP feature that makes it possible to automatically hyphenate, or break, a word that is too long to fit at the end of a line.

Impact Printer—A printer that transfers characters to paper by having an object strike an inked ribbon. Daisywheel and dot-matrix printers fall into this category.

Insert—A WP feature that allows a WP operator to add characters, words, phrases, paragraphs, and even larger blocks of text in between other words or text.

Justification—A WP feature that perfectly aligns right and left margins. In order to justify the right margin, the word processor inserts spaces of various lengths between words on each line, so that all lines appear to be the same length.

Keyboard—The device used to enter data into the word processing system. It is similar in appearance to a standard typewriter keyboard. However, the WP keyboard has some additional keys, called control keys, that can be found above or alongside the standard typing keys.

Modem—A communication device that uses telephone lines to enable computers to communicate with one another.

Monitor—A device, similar to a television screen, that allows you to see a soft copy of your text as it is being keyed into the WP system, but before it is actually printed out.

Nonimpact Printer—A printer that transfers characters to paper without striking an object against an inked ribbon. Instead, characters may be formed by such methods as heat or ink jet (spraying ink onto paper).

Office Automation—The use of computers in office equipment to streamline operations.

Operators—The individuals who run the WP equipment. They are responsible for keying data into the word processor.

Principals—The individuals who originate documents for input into the WP system. They also are referred to as *authors* or *document originators.*

Printer—The device that produces hard copies of your text. Unlike the standard typewriter, the WP printer is generally used only after the document is completed, not throughout the production process.

Random Access Memory (RAM)—WP memory that temporarily stores and handles all information given to the word processor, and can later be erased.

Read Only Memory (ROM)—The WP system's permanent memory. It stores the machine's operating instructions, which tell the CPU how to perform various functions.

Scanner—A unit that digitizes photographs and other illustrations for processing by a computer by using light.

Scrolling—A WP feature that makes possible the upward/downward or left/right movement of text lines so that additional text can be seen on the monitor.

Search—The ability of the WP system to look for a word or group of words that appear in text and to display them on the monitor.

Shared Logic Systems—A category of WP equipment in which several WP terminals share the storage and processing power of one central computer. Unlike stand-alone or distributed logic systems, shared logic terminals are essentially "dumb"–they cannot function without the aid of another computer.

Soft Copy—Text stored in a computer and visible only on a monitor, rather than printed out on paper.

Software—A collection of instructions that once accessed are carried out by a computer.

Spell Check—A WP feature that checks the spelling of the words in a document against the WP system's own internal dictionary.

Stand-Alone Word Processor—A word processor that is totally self-contained. That is, it can function on its own without the aid of another computer.

User Friendly—Easy for a user to understand and operate.

Word Processing—A system of personnel, procedures, and WP equipment that provides efficient and economical printed business communications.

Word Wrap—A WP feature that eliminates the need to hit the return key when you reach the end of a line. Instead, the word processor automatically jumps to the next line when you reach the right margin.

World Wide Web—A part of the Internet that contains sound, animation, video, and graphics.

BIBLIOGRAPHY

Byrne, Joseph J. I-Net+ certification study system. Foster City, CA: IDG Books Worldwide, 2000.

Ceruzzi, Paul E. *A History of Modern Computing.* Cambridge, MA: MIT Press, 1998.

DiSessa, Andrea A. *Changing Minds: Computer, Learning, and Literacy.* Cambridge, MA: MIT Press, 2000.

Duffy, Tim. *Office 2000 Professional.* Reading, MA: Addison Wesley, 1999.

Freedman, Alan. *The Computer Glossary: The Complete Illustrated Dictionary.* American Management Association, 1998.

Frew, Michael. *Learning English Skills Through Word-Processing* (Learning Series Texts). New York: DDC Publishing, 1999.

Gilster, Ron. *A+ Certification for Dummies.* Foster City, CA: IDG Books, 1999.

Jaderstrom, Susan, *et al. The Complete Office Handbook: The Definitive Reference for Today's Electronic Office.* New York: Random House, 1996.

Kaplan, Michael. *Planning and Implementing Technical Services Workstations.* American Library Association, 1997.

Ranadive, Vivek. *The Power of Now: How Winning Companies Sense and Respond to Change Using Real-Time Technology.* New York: McGraw-Hill, 1999.

Stair, Lila B. *Careers in Computers.* Lincolnwood, IL: VGM Career Books, 2002.